BANAH

PERFORMANCE OF A PROMISE . . .

Angie Treadaway

PublishAmerica
Baltimore

© 2003 by Angie Treadaway.
All rights reserved. No part of this book may be reproduced, stored in a retrieval system, or transmitted in any form or by any means without the prior written permission of the publishers, except by a reviewer who may quote brief passages in a review to be printed in a newspaper, magazine, or journal.

First printing

Unless otherwise stated, all Scripture citation is from the King James Version, copyright 1972 by Thomas Nelson Inc.

All Scripture study and word definitions are from Vine's Complete Expository Dictionary of Old and New Testament Words, copyright 1996 by Thomas Nelson Inc. and Commentary on the whole Bible by Matthew Henry, copyright 1961 by Zondervan Publishing House.

Part1, Chapter 3: song "I'm With You," Averil Levigne, 2003.
Part 2, Chapter 5: song "Bobby McGee," Janis Joplin, 1969.
Part 2, Chapter 6: Redbook Magazine, October issue, 2002.
Part 2, Chapter 6: Time Magizine, September issue, 2002.
Part3, Chapter 1: Signs Of Design, by Carl Williland, Copyright

ISBN: 1-59286-867-3
PUBLISHED BY PUBLISHAMERICA, LLLP
www.publishamerica.com
Baltimore

Printed in the United States of America

DEDICATED
TO
CHILDREN
WHO
LONG
FOR
FAMILY
AND ALL CONCRETE ANGELS.

With love and a joy-tear I humbly thank...

...my precious husband, Dan—your quiet strength and gentle, patient love will never be equaled on this earth.

...Brittany—You are the song of my life.

...Lauren-Faith—You are my laughter and my hope.

...Hunter—You are the gentle love of my heart—a priceless reflection of your daddy!

...my mother, Kaye Finley, and my sister, Jessi Hall —It was your house, too. Your love and faith said yes, when I opened the door to our old house in order to bring others to a new one.

...my father—Roger Tutor—You suffered in the house before my house. Our life together enabled me to understand and connect those who remain in the old houses with a promise.

...Mama Dee, Mama Jack, Mama Nan, Mama Tutor, Mamaw, Nan-Nad, J.B. Tutor, Coach Thad Sanders, William Robert and Shirley Mathews, Bruce McCoy, Rusty Cummings, Bob McCustion, Susan Morrow, Grace Martin, Pam, Lynn, Dawn, Rhonda, and Margaret.

...my Friendship family—especially Kay, Shelly, Tiffany, Dawn, Crystal, Gail, Pat, Carolyn, Trudy, Linda, Tracy, Regina, Ramona, Donna, Beth, Peggy, Synthia, Neva, Jackie,-- without your prayers, I couldn't live!

* Glenda—you somehow deciphered my mess and turned my drafts into something readable! You're the best!

> I love you all so much! Each one used by the.
> Master to help me reach true normal.
> **May God bless and keep you forever!**

◆TABLE OF CONTENTS◆

PART 1: THE OLD NEIGHBORHOOD

CHAP 1: THE HOUSE VOID OF WARMTH AND LOVE	10
CHAP 2: THE HOUSE OF FEAR	15
CHAP 3: THE EMPTY HOUSE	21
CHAP 4: THE HOUSE WITH THE FORBIDDEN ROOM	29
CHAP 5: THE HOUSE OF BROKEN GIFTS	33
CHAP 6: THE HOUSE OF THE PRETTY PURPLE DRESS	36

PART II: DEMOLITION, REMODELING, AND ARCHITECTURAL DESIGN

CHAP 1: "NORMAL" FAÇADE	41
CHAP 2: A DISSERTATION ON CLOGGED PLUMBING	48
CHAP 3: BEAMS OF SECURITY ON FOUNDATIONS OF PEACE	51
CHAP 4: THE LAMP IN THE DEN	56
CHAP 5: CALL SANFORD AND SON!	62
CHAP 6: WINDOWS TO THE SOUL	71
CHAP 7: APPRAISAL NOT REQUIRED!	78

PART III: THE NEW NEIGHBORHOOD

CHAP 1: THE ULTIMATE ARCHITECT	81
CHAP 2: MAINTENANCE AND UPKEEP	87
CHAP 3: THE HOUSE WITH THE STEEPLE	91
CHAP 4: UNRIVALED SOUTHERN HOSPITALITY	94
CHAP 5: "WE DWELL IN HIM"	103

Part 1:

INTRODUCTION

Memories of childhood visit me at odd times. I've heard the stories of people who cannot remember the past. It seems they have erased those years, and nothing remains but a blank space in time. I've never done that. I can picture those days vividly, as if it were only yesterday. What would have been my blank space has been redesigned and transformed. Those memories do not haunt me. Instead they cause an awesome moment of worship for the one who transformed them into joy. The transformation all began with a long ago prayer. As a little girl in the old neighborhood, I asked God for a family. I said please. I asked Him for a home.

I didn't know it then, but there was a promise in the Bible. This promise was made by God, and it is simply this: "I will build thee a house." I have come to realize that to ask God for a family and home is asking for the performance of a spoken promise. Results will occur. When God speaks, things move. Situations change. Life changes. I have lovingly begun to call this promise the Banah promise. Banah is the ancient Hebrew word used in scriptures when God established the first family by forming Eve from Adam's rib (Genesis 2:22). Banah is used again in 2 Samuel as God promises David that He, God, would build David's house.

When I prayed as a child, there was never any doubt about results. Leaving the old houses has been a long journey. But God brought me out. He promised. I prayed. It works.

My story of Banah starts many years ago in an old neighborhood, down memory lane. Travel with me. We must go back there to see exactly how God worked in my house. If you've already left your old neighborhood, maybe Banah will help you understand how it took place, and then you can help someone else leave. If you're still living in these houses, I want you to claim the Banah Promise as your own today. God builds a family and a home. He has promised, and He will build yours. You take this journey with me, be open to faith and trust, and I promise you, your house will be built.

Part 1 - Chapter 1

THE HOUSE VOID OF WARMTH AND LOVE

A child looks out the window for the fifth time in an afternoon and sighs deeply. Every trip to the window has been hopeful, and every trip back to the couch has been wishful. *Maybe the next one will be them*, she thinks to herself. She hears a faint noise in the distance. *Is it a car? It could be! Yes!* She dashes to the window just in time to see the red Pinto pull into the drive.

"They're here!" Another swift dash to the door – but suddenly she stops – thinking again – and instead of running, she waits across the room. Very quietly, she watches the door to the house that is her home. Several moments pass by and the door opens. The faces she's been waiting for appear. Faces she's longed for throughout the day. Those she loves are now near, but they don't see her. Life is in the way. Cautiously, she observes the faces and listens to the voices before moving. Her heart wants to run to them, but her mind tells her to be still. Her every thought and action in their presence is carefully calculated. You see, some days there is freedom to run and jump into their arms with giggles or kisses. Some days, a wall of life's layers towers between them, and to run and jump would mean a painful impact with solid layers of bitterness and harshness. This house is the first house on Banah's memory lane. I call it the House Void of Warmth and Love.

Many more people than we could ever imagine have never lived in a house filled with warm love. As I listen to stories of friends and acquaintances, it takes me back to a time when I was the child waiting in the shadows of the long afternoon above.

In those shadow memories, I can still feel the warm flow of love welling up in my heart. A continuous steady stream flowed outward toward the faces in my house. The warm love desperately wanted to wrap around my loved ones and make right whatever was so terribly wrong in their lives. We are all born with warm love in our hearts. The ability to love, and the desire to be loved is God's plan and purpose for his beloved.

Many, however, learned very early in life that the warm flow from the heart had to be measured and controlled – stifled at times – and stopped altogether at others. Waiting across a room, reading the gauges of a face or the tone of a voice, we carefully calculated the "run with giggles" versus "the retreat to our room." More often than not, those faces would not receive our flow of love. Would not? Or was it *could not*?

Generational layers of life were firmly in place long before many of us were born. These were layers of wrong actions based on wrong responses to wrong patterns of thinking. They were generational attitudes and interactions between family members. The people trapped in the layers usually knew no other way of life. When people have never seen true "normal," then they've never felt the warm, the secure, the beautiful free love that is God's plan for every house. I don't believe any person would NOT receive warm love if they had ever truly known it. Therefore, I believe many generations CANNOT because they KNOW NOT. (He that loveth not knoweth not…) With every new generation, the layers become more solid and the bitterness increases. Children are still waiting and watching from the shadows. For this reason, my heart is stirred to find these families and carry warmth to them, warmth that contains a very special spoken promise.

As the small child learns to contain the love, holding it carefully inside, what do you suppose happens to the child's chest? There is a lump that forms right in the center, where the heart is. If love cannot flow, the child grows up with a serious condition that I call "clogged plumbing". The condition is passed from generation to generation unless something powerful is applied to the chest to dissolve the lump. For me, that powerful something was understanding the love of God. Living in a house void of warmth and love has given me precious insight that I might otherwise have never known. You see, as we loved, and loved so deeply, and that love was not received – we received an intimate knowledge of the suffering affection of God for His beloved. If we think carefully, there is a way to connect the way we loved them to the way He loves us. The word "suffer" comes from the Greek work "proseao". It means "to let" or "permit' – "permit further". In a house void of warmth and love, we were experiencing a truth of God so very early in life: Loving in spite of the actions or responses of those we loved. We said in our hearts, "Whatever you do, I still will love you, for that is all I know how to do!" The chest in those moments began to become clogged with a huge lump of suffering affection.

Jesus loves the children in this house so tenderly. He is the suffering Savior who knew suffering affection all the way to the call of the cross. He's the One waiting and watching His beloved receive anything and everything but the love He offers. His timeless message has always been the same – "I will permit you to do whatever you do – and I still will love you – for that is what I AM." He waits in the shadows of our house and in the quietness of our days. He observes with sadness in our darkest nights. He holds back warm, flowing love because we don't understand how much He loves! He waits to be wanted by the ones He lives for! Suffering love in immense, patient abundance!

"Passion" is a word that makes us think of an extreme, intense love – vivid – burning with color and emotion – blazing with a life of it s own. The Greek word for passion is "pathema". Pathema's definition is "suffering affection". God's passion was the cross. Suffering to the sacrifice to release the power to get the loved to the beloved. There was no avoiding the suffering, for it made a way to release the love to me and you!

The pure, willing to be wronged just to be near you love that so many of us knew in our hearts as children has enabled me to understand God's passion for His beloved creation. If you have never known a house filled with warmth and love, please turn your thoughts to this truth. Let the understanding of His precious warm love soak into your mind and heart. Refuse to live in a house void of warm love another day. You do not have to control the flow ever again. He loves us the way we loved them. We can love freely, and be confident and secure in the passion we are receiving in return.

God's passion for me moved me to a new house absolutely filled with warm love. His careful work in my chest started when I understood the Love who wanted my love, more than I could comprehend. There will be no new house until His love is understood and your door is opened to receive it. We must stop striving for a response from the people in our house. We must stop placing expectations on the people in our house. Whether generational layers, or simply because we're human, people will never completely meet our needs or fulfill our expectations. We have great needs and great expectations – all of us. God's passion waits to meet and fulfill them. Nothing else will. Nothing else should.

> *Yea, I have loved thee with an everlasting love –*
> *Therefore, I have drawn thee with loving kindness*
> *–Again, I will build thee, and thou shalt be built!*
> *Jeremiah 31: 3-4*

The spoken promise to build begins with endless, measureless, warm love that draws the beloved with kindness – loving kindness. He'll take your heart, locked in your chest with the flow of warmth you guard there. He'll hold it in His warm hands and His loving kindness will surround, and permeate, and hold, and nurture the gauges you've so carefully placed around it away! No more walking on eggshells.

God is drawing you, my precious friend, with loving kindness that has stretched from the beginning of the ages. His suffering affection is revealed in the passion of the Cross. He promises throughout scripture to build His beloved. I long to reach through the words of these pages and lead your heart to the warmth of the Master's hands – the Master Artificer – the Ultimate Architect.

We will travel on and visit the other houses on Banah's memory lane, for God is in the business of whole new neighborhoods. If your desire is a new house, there is something I will ask you to do: Pray this prayer – whisper it – think it – meditate on it –

Lord,

    The house void of warmth and love aches. The fullness of my chest, so clogged with the love that wanted to flow to them is sometimes choking me! Lord, make me a new house – I don't want to rent or borrow – I want to own! I know now that I am forever beloved. Build my house, Lord, please build my house!

Now read Jeremiah 31:4 again.

Again, I will build thee, and thou shalt be built.

Wow!

Part 1 - Chapter 2

THE HOUSE OF FEAR

The next house on Banah's memory lane is the "House of Fear." A terrible generational pattern lived here. Many people with normal faces lived here. They were frozen in this house. They were frozen in its grip. Many times a well-meaning church is what held them there. I want to make one thing very clear in this book. If you live in the House of Fear today, you don't have to stay. My heart wants you to know there is a way out. It requires delicate and intricate soul work. But the work will be done by very warm and capable hands. The only hands capable of repairing the damaged dynamics of control and cruelty. My family lived far too long in this house, because the understanding was that one did not divorce, no matter what. God does hate divorce. So do I. It hurts. But God also hates to see the weak trampled, and the innocent living in fear, captive and abused. He hates for the children to learn the patterns and repeat the mistakes in their own house. My parents were not born responding to life in these awful explosions of loudness and anger – they were taught. When a couple is told to stay together, God help us remember to teach them how.

In the House of Fear, we began our lives responding in innocence and trust to the people in our house as we grew from a baby into childhood. Innocence always has a wide, gaping smile for those around it. Innocence does not judge or hold accountable. It looks at others through eyes filled with unconditional love – and wants to laugh with those it sees. Innocence is simple. It is unmixed with things foreign to warm love.

Then, innocence gradually became aware of crashes in the night – loud, frightening sounds jolting us awake – drawing us from our bed – poised – running – ready to instinctively protect those we loved. We reached their room, and the protective instinct is thwarted and frustrated, because innocence loves the one who needs protection as much as the one protection is needed from!

Then we were told, "Go back to bed!...Now!"

We ran back to bed – pulled the blankets up to our eyes – and we lay there listening to muffled screams, foul and hate-filled accusations with whimpered denials. We'd lie so very still, eyes wide and tense, and innocence was frantically and violently introduced to fear. We couldn't know then that our beloved had known the same introduction many years before. The sounds were out of control – the voices were out of control – the anger was out of control – everything in the night would begin to spin and spin terribly out of control!

Our lives were changed as innocence cowered in fear. This kind of fear causes the very foundation of our lives to become agitated and unsettled. With an unsettled foundation, our soul was cast forever downward from a sense of security, and there in the foundation, far away from secure, we became the family of fear's closest relatives – dread and apprehension. Fear, dread, and apprehension at once worked together to block any introduction at all to peace and gentleness. We didn't miss peace. We had never known it. Dread became the funny, drawing, sick feeling in the stomach that surfaces in adulthood for no apparent reason. The result is usually a withdrawal from all people, even those closest to you. Apprehension surfaces as an expectation of the worst in all situations, and often suspiciously mistaking the good intentions of good people for bad. The House of Fear affects the very foundation of our entire life. The results may not surface until adulthood, but they will surface, and this damaged foundation must be faced in order to move out and move on.

We lay there on those nights and loved them both so deeply. And there, in the deepest darkness of those nights, the innocent child transformed – becoming the grief-stricken, weathered, child/parent of two people lost in a house void of warm love, a house of fear, a house without hope. Day by day, and night by night, generational patterns of family life were taught to us by those we watched and loved from a distance. And we always watched with eyes full of suffering affection. It was a sort of "home-schooling!". The curriculum included how to apply heavy make-up around the eyes and mouth, how to plan and give elaborate persuasive speeches for friends and family to explain the obvious, and how to play the wonderful game we are all experts at– "pretending it never happened." We learned how to cover huge wrongs with extreme perfection. Before long, the wrongs were so expertly covered, they didn't seem wrong anymore. Just normal. And no other kind of life was understood as possible for those who lived there.

I don't believe it glorifies the Father to be any more detailed at this point except to say that, but for the grace of God, one of my beloved would have killed the other. My heart is crying for those of you "child/parents" who did suffer through this house to that end.

Then one day we grew a little older, and the anger turned. Just as the crashes and screams had jolted us from our sleep, solid blows began to jolt us backward – addling our senses for a few moments – not hurting at first because we're stunned – then wet, hot, salty tears would run into the corners of our mouths. I remember the saltiness mingled with the hurt. But the child/parent continues only to want the wrongs to be made right! We agreed the punishment was deserved if that meant we could be near them! Hello suffering affection! At this point, one of the beloved may weakly protest, but years of wrongs put blinders on people! They've lived in this house until there is no memory of 'right', and any other kind of house is vague, distant, and unfamiliar.

One of the first things we must learn about the "House of Fear" is that something was planted deep within us during those long, dark hours of childhood:

> *The child grew, and waxed strong in spirit,* and was in the deserts until the day of his showing unto Israel.
> *Luke 1:80*

The child "remaining" in the desert, deprived of normal comforts in a solitary uninhabitable wilderness – will advance, or become strong! Deep inside a child living in the House of Fear became a person with the scruples needed to survive and move on! You are strong, beloved! Layers of circumstances in your life may have you convinced that there is <u>no</u> <u>way</u> <u>out</u>. But a survival strength was developed in those uninhabitable nights that will enable you to have a different life! The abused believes leaving is impossible. But leaving is both possible and required until the abuser seeks help and soul repair takes place. The abuser's promise is <u>not</u> acceptable. The abuser's search for Godly counsel and definite, measurable, life-changing results over a long period of time is acceptable. The abuser believes change is impossible. But change is a promise spoken by Love to all who will hear. Change is a new house in a new neighborhood. The abused – the abuser – and those caught in between are strong! God's passion is present – and His warm hands can still the hands of violence and soften the loudness and stop the spin. God designed us from birth so that life in the desert would cause the strength to reach for something better! It caused the strength to reach for His warm hands! This child/parent waxed strong! The desert made me able to reach! – withstand and reach! – competent and determined to break the cycle. . The strength of the desert made possible what otherwise would not have been possible – leaving the House of Fear for good.

Precious friend, you must use your strength. You must take action! – Take back the things evil has considered its own prize up to this point in your life, and with all the strength of your being, let evil's desired prize be transformed at the foot of the Cross into the glory of the Father's love! Take captive every memory that causes you to feel hurt, hate, resentment, regret, or self-pity and say to God, "I give it to you! Use it to reveal more strength!" Do not give in to those thoughts and use them as an excuse for repeating the same mistakes! Ask God to break through the layers of generational cycles in your house beginning right now!

Innocent love wanted to help – but we could only lie in the dark as our beloved hurt each other for hours upon hours, upon hours, upon hours…..Nobody lives in the "House of Fear" without damage to the foundation of the soul. We respond to everything in our lives from that foundation. I've noticed there are two very predictable changes that seem to touch the lives of every one of us who've lived in a "House of Fear." One is that <u>we develop an extremely aggressive or extremely passive nature. Very rarely will we have a good balance of our emotional responses. Extreme abuse may not be present, but verbal lashing and verbal abuse of our spouse and children can surface and rip our homes apart. And remember, words do not have to be loud to become word bullets. They can flow softly and sound sweet, yet deliver death to the spirit they fall into. The second predictable change is the inability to confront a problem or issue in the workplace without tears or extreme agitation and anger which will limit our successes professionally. A shaky foundation is revealed quickly when pressure increases in even the smallest amounts.</u>

To feel powerless and frozen in this "House of Fear" is not acceptable any more. We have waxed strong. God has spoken a promise to build a new house. Draw on that strength, turn your eyes on the promise of God, and invite Him into your "House of Fear."

When we get to part II of Banah, I'll tell you how He worked in my "House of Fear" – it was a marvelous construction site! In the meantime, prepare for great and glorious changes in you as we head in that direction. Pray, my friend, pray this prayer, now:

Lord,
    Where did it begin?
    The loudness, the anger, the violence, the threats, the name-calling, the explosions of trust and love that shattered the houses?

    Why did it begin, Lord?
    Down deep, it seems it was a cry from the unloved– all along.
    Explosively demanding love and trust– demanding some kind of healing.
    Threatening their beloved for not giving what they called for.

Damaging all that could have loved or trusted or helped to heal.

Only you, Lord, can break the cycle. Only you can change generational patterns of life, and rebuild the houses.

Your gentleness – Your peace –Strength quiet enough to build my house. I need you so, Lord.

Amen

O thou afflicted, tossed with tempest, and not comforted, Behold–I will lay thy stones with fair colors And lay thy <u>foundations</u> with sapphires….. And great <u>shall</u> be the <u>peace</u> <u>of thy</u> <u>children</u>.

Isaiah 54: 11-13

(i.e. generational cycle broken)

Wow!

Part 1 - Chapter 3

THE EMPTY HOUSE

We'll go now and look into what my heart calls "The Empty House." You'll know the one…nobody's home. Countless numbers of us spent so many days and nights alone. If someone asked, we said we were "fine." But at 2 and 3 A.M., we could be found lying in the dark with the blankets pulled up to our eyes – and this time the fear was different. The blankets were now there to hide us from things that go *bump* in the night. We lay hour after hour, hearing every creak and pop, every faint noise in the house. We know the darkness of one night can seem to last forever. The hours crept by, and I can remember actually breathing more easily when the dawn would begin to break.

Some mornings, when the light would begin to peep around the window's edge, I would literally whisper, "Thank you God! I made it!" It never bothered me that I didn't sleep. I was just happy to "make it" through the dark! The child/parent is often tired. The long night vigils take their toll!

I know the first impulse can be to shower the child with words of encouragement about how life should be. We are so anxious to rush them right into warmth and love. But a different kind of house is foreign to them, and the child/parent would feel awkward and clumsy. Yes, that's the word – "clumsy" – being rushed into a new house. They must be gently led and allowed time to follow as they find grace. Too many words spoken against the house they live in can sound condemning, and warm is not trusted when mixed with condemnation.

In the "Empty House," the night-time is dreaded and long. The fear is compounded, but the child/parent will refuse to be taken elsewhere. There's just something unexplainable about home; we long to be there, in *our* home, no matter the circumstance.

There is another type of "Empty House." As we look inside, there are warm bodies present, but the child lives alone. The child of an addict saw the beloved spend hour after hour on the living room couch or in the bed. Physical sickness was the blame, but spiritual sickness would have been a more accurate diagnosis. In this "Empty House," another home-schooling lesson of the child/parent is learned – to excuse all wrong behavior by giving sympathy and aid to the physical symptoms, and <u>NEVER</u> address the fact that the most logical path to wellness would be to leave off the toxin! The child in this house waits patiently for a few cherished moments when their beloved has clear eyes and a free smile. To the child, those moments are worth a lifetime of waiting.

And lastly, there's the "Empty House" occupied by – to be honest – "parent/child." In this house, the adults were consumed with personal interests, and all responsibility was laid aside. The child became extra baggage, too cumbersome to pursue dreams. There was a lot of shame the child of this house experienced upon accidentally walking into a room where there was no welcome. Especially if the child stumbled into the territory of the beloved's new love. Many of us believed this was legitimate – and if we were in the way – we were sorry! We did our very best to become such a perfect child it would make them want to include us in their new life.

Ladies, if you became skinny, beautiful, smart – not "needing" anything, you would not be too cumbersome, and you could be near them! Men, if you became tough, fast, rich – they would be proud of you and include you in their life they shared with others.

Some did not believe this was legitimate, and the dislike of the beloved grew daily. Anger and resentment became statements such as, "He is not my father!" or "She is crazy!", "I don't need them!, I'm fine without them!", "When I turn 18, I'm gone!", "I hope I never see them again!", "I hate him!", "I hate her!" The trick here was to convince ourselves and everyone around us that we did not "need", and we were incredible masters of disguise!

The houses on Banah's memory lane give us a predictable pattern of a child parent's development of personality, character, thought processes, and responses. The patterns were developed as a means of coping and of surviving – but they will cause the adult child/parent to live behind a false façade. Masters of disguise attempting normal life from behind a false presentation of a self who loves deeply and has incredible need. It is a struggle to live alongside other families in truth, because so many have never seen real truth in a house! We grow into adult child/parents, and our façade appears "normal," but it disguises the structural damage on the inside threatening collapse!

I made all of those statements – I believed in my own heart that I did not need my parents or a "regular" home. I convinced all of my friends that having the house to myself was free and fun! I made a pact with myself to take care of myself. I convinced myself not to need – ever – for the only way to get up and go to school or work every day was to do it in spite of the need. This worked. And life was 'normal' to all who knew me.

But I told my friends I had to be home by eleven, because I knew other girls had a curfew. They never knew I arrived home at eleven to an empty house.

And somewhere in the back of my mind there was always a faint picture of a den, with a lamp turned on, and my parents together, sitting on a couch, watching TV, waiting for me. When thinking of the empty houses, I recall a special part of my earliest understanding of faith. Jesus said, "Let the children come to Me." Oh, how I love Jesus! And how deeply He loves the heart of His child. As young as 3 or 4 years of age, I can remember praying. My great-grandmother taught me, "When you finish praying, you say, not my will, Father, but Your will be done." Then you say, "in Jesus' name, Amen." "That's how God hears your prayers, is when you say, 'in Jesus' name'." She would pat my hand and say, "Even a child is known by his doings. When nobody else can see you, God can see you, no matter where you are!" The Word sent out of my precious great-grandmother could not return void! No way! God said it would not! God bless the grandmothers and grandfathers in this world who are unable to follow their beloved grandchild into the house, but day by day they cover the child in prayer and share with them a promise at every chance afforded!

When alone, I remembered what she said. When in the grip of fear, I talked to Him! Mama Tutor said He knew where I was. So I asked Him not to let them die – I prayed, "Please don't let anything get me!" "Please let daylight hurry up and come!" And guess what? Nothing got me, they did not die, and the daylight always came. Thank you Father! The child acquainted with suffering affection and living in an Empty House developed a believing heart. I believed God was there, and when I spoke those prayers, He heard me! There was absolutely no doubt in my mind. "Even a child is known" meant to me that God knew where I was. I understood I was never alone. A child's heart readily accepts faith without a need to be convinced.

Can you trust with a child's heart? To move from the "Empty House," Dear One, you must come to understand God's presence in your house. When God spoke of His presence in our life, it meant this:

Now
Just now
In this very moment
The face of God –
The countenance –
The part towards the eyes
Which by its various movements
Gives you an index
Of inward thoughts –
Or feelings –
Towards you –
That part… …
Is before you.

Get it? His presence is His face always before you with eyes that are filled with love – eyes that long for you to tell Him of your need! Oh, praise Him!

In the bedroom of that empty house, there was a little girl talking to the Creator of the Universe. His face was turned to her in every moment! A little girl with a believing heart was living in the presence of a majestic King!

You must grasp with everything in you and hold tightly to the fact that the One who gives you breath *is present* in the room with you! He is present when you're at work or school, when you're in the old houses, when you're in the darkest moments of your life! And when asked, He *will* give you the power to change your life!

From this day forward, no more accepting things the way they are. No more hoping it will be better 'someday'! Your someday is *now*!

Just now.
In this moment.
In His presence!
Imagine His eyes!
Believe in His passion for you!
Understand, to live at all is to live in His presence.

The next part is critical. It is vital! You must talk! It is <u>not enough</u> to <u>know</u> He's there. You *must* take action and speak your need to Him. Layers and layers of experiences and circumstances may cause you to pause here at this point of your journey. The layers will seem to be "between" you and God and you don't believe He will hear you talking. But you *must* understand: His love–His suffering affection– BECAME the layers. And Love's POWER – it "exploded" out of that sacrifice! The power of the sacrifice of Love is able to permeate every layer until all that is before Him is the precious soul to which He is giving life!! You begin to apply <u>that power to your layers</u> when you begin to talk!

The first thing you say is -
"God, I *need* you."
Then,
"God, I *want* you."

When I started talking to Him, I didn't know big words, or denominational doctrines! I just *NEEDED*! At every crook and turn of my journey – I *NEEDED*! When I spoke that "need" to His countenance – to His presence– the *POWER* of His sacrifice BLASTED the layers of life away! I was before a Holy Father with a Huge loving heart, who in that moment, began to build my house!

Please – speak your heart to Him, dear one! Tell Him of your need! Tell Him you want life to be different!

I want to address something else before we go further. If I asked God for a family when I was four years old, and I asked for the layers to stop when I was five and six years old, why, some will ask, would a loving God not answer the believing heart of a child if there is so much passion there?

I say to you, thank God, it is because there IS SO MUCH PASSION THERE!! God has shown me this so carefully! – Lord, - please let me carefully share it!

Love is gentle.
Love will not force itself.
This is the law of love, and God is love.
To become the sons and daughters of the God of love,
we must accept that His patient suffering love was also
extended to our "parent/children" as they frustrated and
terribly distorted this law of love by refusing it.
Love was reaching for them, the same as love is reaching
for you and me.
It must, because It is!

But love was never willing that we should suffer alone! Love entered into a life on earth to suffer with us! – He did bleed! – He wore the sharp and painful crown! – He was stabbed, and the fluids from His body ran down His side! – He was nailed, and as He gave His perfect, innocent life, at that point in time, the Holiness of the Godhead couldn't look at His own love! Because at that moment in time, He became every bitter thing! – Every molestation. – Every painful blow. – Every scream. – Every horror in evil's capacity. – Jesus became!! He knew all the darkness we have ever known. Love felt and faced it all – and in doing so <u>released</u> the power and the strength for us to feel and face what we must. He was with me at age 4, 5, 6, and 9–and He is with me *now*! Love knew what I had to know–and love has never left my side. Not yours, either. Whatever you've lived through, Jesus bore it in His sacrifice. This is why you do need.– You need HIM!! He's the One who does understand, and has the POWER for you to face it, deal with it, overcome it, and use it. *He experienced it to defeat it.*

> *Christ suffered for us, leaving us an example, that we should follow in His steps: Who did no sin – Neither was guile found in his mouth: Who, <u>when He was reviled, reviled not again</u>; <u>When He suffered, He threatened not</u>; <u>But committed Himself to God</u>. Who His own self <u>bare our sins in His own body</u> on the tree, <u>that we could overcome the sin and its effects on our life</u> (interpretation mine) – For <u>by His stripes we are healed</u>!*

1 Peter 2: 21-24

And while young, love was there. Love stands beside you *now*. Love has the answers. Dear precious friend, ask Him today. Know Love in *His* fullness!! Let Him give you the keys to life. Speak your heart to Him. Close this book and talk!

I promise you –
    You are <u>not</u> alone.
        He's present.
            And,
                He's listening!!!

I heard a song on the radio recently, and as it played, my heart heard a generation of people living in empty houses. The song writer must have spent some time at my house as a child! I found myself answering each line as I drove along:

I'm waitin' in the dark – (DON'T BE AFRAID!)

I thought you'd be here by now (HE IS!)
I'm listening but there's no sound (LISTEN WITH YOUR HEART!)
I'm looking for a place (LOOK WITH YOUR HEART!)
Searching for a face (OH, THE COUNTENANCE!)
Is anybody here I know (HE KNOWS YOU!)
Cause nothing's going right
And everything's a mess
And no one likes to be alone (TELL ME ABOUT IT!)
Isn't anyone tryin' to find me? (YES!)
Won't somebody come take me home?? (A NEW HOUSE!)
I don't know who you are (IT'S LOVE HIMSELF!)
But I.....I'm with you.....

Oh, if only this song, were a prayer to the Love that is giving us breath! The sadness and the desolate need heard in the melody would be changed into an awesome understanding of never being alone again! I will never be alone again. God, as for me, I......I'm with you......

Part 1 - Chapter 4

THE HOUSE OF THE FORBIDDEN ROOM

A "House of the Forbidden Room" is now seen in America's neighborhoods and towns on every block – and, quite probably, every ten-mile stretch of highway. When today's adult child/parents were young, these houses were fewer and more scattered. I've personally been surprised by neighbors who now live in this house because it is no longer dictated by geographical or economical confines. Regardless of the statistics, the children in this house are still the same. Experiences in the "House of the Forbidden Room" can only be addressed with love, prayer, and careful balance, if one is to gain a child/parent's trust – and attempt to create a concrete way to move out and move on. Once again – it can mean the difference between a life of joy or despair, health or sickness, and, eventually, life or death.

In this house there was a room forbidden, "off limits," to us as we played. Innocence never questioned this rule – we'd just go around it. The room was used most often by those who entered our life as our heroes. This part of the family loved a party! In an otherwise dark and dreary sort of life – these people brought the fun! When we were very young – and living in the various houses of our neighborhood, we looked so forward to being in this house! There was music and food and laughter… but wait a minute – did I mention, "party"?

You might remember them – the parties that lasted most of the night, with loud music and lots of smoke. It was "fun." I spent hours sitting on the floor in front of the amplifier (the loudest speaker) of my dad's band. They cranked out "Freebird" and "Honky Tonk Woman" and I loved it! It was incredible, loud, free, fun!

"Fun", that is, for a little while. The combination of people, alcohol, smoke, dance, and guns was very volatile. Late in the night, unexpected twists would cause fear and apprehension in the very young, but after a while only shoulder shrugs from the older "child/parents"! The hardness of emotions is not hard to explain here.

Clogged plumbing says it all. I believe these nights may explain why so many of us cringe at the thought of guns in our house. Protection is needed! And I promise you, this is NOT a plug *for* or *against* gun control – it is a statement about growing up near those who waved guns around in alcohol-fueled rages. We shrink away because we've watched through tired, young eyes the exact opposite of "responsible use". Both sides of the gun control issue should carefully remember the little people who've been silently watching for years.

Not only were our eyes carefully observing the fun that ended in fear – we were watching the use of the forbidden room by our heroes. Somewhere along the way I figured out that whatever was in the forbidden room made a big change in "fun". It made a big change in 'hero'. And, it had the power to steal life away from all who used it.

During play with other kids, someone would inevitably stumble into the forbidden room. Jumping or stepping over newspaper laid in the floor with plants scattered across it was a game of hopscotch! A neighbor's child would ask, "What's that?" – Another would say, "I don't know." The child of this house usually pretends not to know. We played "water-guns" with syringes. Pipes, tubes, and bongs all became just another make-believe wand, magic trick, or whatever imagination invented that day!

There were also strange smells, we noticed, coming from that room. And the happy, fun heroes in our life would become very sleepy and quiet. Once asleep, you couldn't wake them! At least not until late in the following day – and then they weren't so nice and fun – they were sluggish and mean, and the strange smells always lingered.

Some nights the cops would come suddenly. All of your loved ones, including you, would be required to stand in a circle while the policeman asked your name and shined a flashlight in your face. Other cops would go searching through the house. All you could do was stand there and *hope* against hope your loved ones made it out the back window before they were caught! In our world, we learned cops were "bad" and/or "wrong". You breathed a jagged breath of relief when the loved ones got away. You grieved with the pain and worry of the aged when you saw them handcuffed, put into the cop car, and taken away!

The hurting inside the heart grips and squeezes you – speechless – heart pounding, tears – seeing those handcuffs on your beloved – oh, how you *wanted* to explain that they *really weren't bad people! They were good!* You wanted to help them and promise the cops they really had it all wrong!

By God's marvelous grace and mercy, I did not become a keeper of the forbidden room. Incidentally, not one of my family members who "kept" this room is still alive. They died very young. They died addicted. Their way of life really had taken away my loved ones long before their physical deaths. As they approached the age of 30, these heroes had spaced out – blank stares. They couldn't hold jobs. Their hands shook. The free smiles they had given me as a younger child became strained. They had begun to foolishly steal from anyone in the family that was careless enough not to lock their doors and hide their belongings.

We, the children, watched them waste away beautiful, gifted lives. We understood, quite stoically, that life was not a week-long party. Nothing was 'fun' when the party ended – and there was absolutely nothing we could do to save them. So we walked away. It was our only choice.

It's one of the hardest things we ever do – that point in which we have to go on with our own lives, and leave the beloved behind.

This makes them mad. They call you a snob – and discuss you as if you are a traitor. You "think you're too good" for them.

But that's not true. Not really. Suffering affection will always be in our hearts.

Some child/parents can't take being criticized and ostracized by those they've loved so long from afar. So they stay and become the "keeper" of the Forbidden Room. The money's great…and the popularity… It all goes with the territory when you're the life of the party…

And another one bites the dust way too soon. Suffering affection to the point of losing your life. Make the connection, friend. I'm thinking maybe you could begin to really understand the love of our God who watches His beloved waste the precious gifts of life and fun on a high that falls way too fast. <u>He sees the heroes take in the substances that drain His gifts from their very beings!</u> Yes! God loves us this very same way we've loved them! *He left the throne to make the sacrifice, to **release** the **power**, to **break** the **addictions**!* To the adult child/parent or the "child" – those who are users, keepers, or watchers of the Forbidden room – the "junk room" of all rooms! – THE ROOM NO LONGER HAS POWER TO STEAL LIFE AWAY WHEN CONFRONTED WITH THE LIFE-GIVING POWER OF THE CROSS!!

In part two of this book – we'll invite God into this house – the God who offered the *ultimate sacrifice*. We'll call Sanford and Son – and the junk in the forbidden room will be hauled to the dump! – A house where life was wasted will become a house where life is vibrant, strong, and whole!

Part 1 - Chapter 5

THE HOUSE OF BROKEN GIFTS

Still another house is the one with closets filled with "adult" magazines or videos. The house where the child/parent's parent-child says things like, "You can't hide the world from them," and the other parent-child says, "You're wrong," but then does nothing to prevent access to the material. Do you notice how the "adults" viewing and using "adult" materials have no deep "adult" trust and pure "adult" bonds with the precious souls in their house? They *daily* lose the ability to experience adult joy and establish adult bonds with anyone, because their lives are consumed with *false* bonds they have formed with something that is *not real*. Meanwhile, the child/parent has a curiosity about sexuality that God built into them. (Physical intimacy WAS God's idea after all!) So, with innocent eyes, the six- and seven-year-olds became acquainted with the world's sexuality one day at a time! Listen, dear friends in the faith, this house is to be GRIEVED for! Oh, how the enemy loves to see powerful, gut wrenching, twisting and distortion of God's gifts!! How often is this gift ripped open too soon and exchanged for cheap reproductions! – Twisted into forms unrecognizable when compared to the original intent of its Creator! If this house is a secret part of the life you've lived, please don't hide it behind the "rights" in your life! God's power needs to confront, deal with, correct, heal, and reform EVERYTHING twisted by the enemy! There is COMPLETE victory in the Blood of the Lamb! Don't you ever doubt it!

The House of Broken Gifts is especially sinister in its ability to twist and mangle God's precious gift of intimacy. Many sexually abused or sexually addicted Christian adults have looked at me through tear-filled eyes – with genuine hurt and confusion – asking, "Why was there a response?"

Listen, precious friend – interest, desire, and curiosity about this gift was placed in us by a magnificent Master Designer – a gift to us for our marriage – to be experienced with joy! It is placed in us to make our lives with our spouses complete, whole, and right! Our young minds had no way of knowing that the images taken in were not what the Master Designer had intended for the opening of the gift! For every one of us, He had created that special one to seal our lives with. His plan was always to give us a complete and priceless gift for us to experience in our marriage. It is an intimacy with such richness and depth that <u>no images on screen or paper will ever be able to capture it!</u> Screen and paper can be altered, painted, fabricated and arranged. Relational depth and relational intimacy are true and pure! There are no imitations for this part of the gift! There is no way to buy it or fake it!

Who is explaining this to 8, 10, and 12-year-olds with access to pornographic material? I've seen many adults saying, "no" or "bad," while sneaking a smile about what's hidden in their own houses!

Christians, come clean! The things you view are affecting your lives today! Not only did young minds learn to respond to false images, the young hearts made the connection that those images do not expect anything in return!

> Images in the mind form a barrier to the soul that will stand between a husband and wife for a lifetime if the broken gift is not brought before our God. We must lay our soul before Him – allowing Him to restore us!!!

Many marriages end today because adult child/parents who lived in this house continue relational intimacy with the images in their mind rather than looking outside and into the eyes of their spouse. For most, to move out of this house will seem an impossible task. To speak about this subject in prayer to a Holy God is the last thing you feel you can do! But humbled, honest, on your knees time in His presence is the only thing that will move you! Note the word HONEST. Absolutely nothing is in your head that He doesn't already know. The broken gift begins to be restored when you honestly bring it back to Him, lay it down, and allow Him to work in the <u>specifics</u> of where <u>your gift</u> <u>has</u> <u>personally</u> <u>been</u>!

There are many different ways your gift could have been affected, broken and misused. But there is only one Maker of the gift who is able to repair it, restore it and teach us to use it to all of its glorious and wonderful potential, the way it was intended from the beginning of your life!

The House of Broken Gifts is looming and sinister! It is the one for many of us that is the hardest to get out of because of the guilt and shame involved. Please don't stop here! Continue with me as we walk through this neighborhood – and when we arrive at Part II of Banah, I pray our Father will be preparing you to truly trade spaces – truly let Him inside this House and let the *power* of HIS SACRIFICE leave you *speechless*!!! You must be preparing your heart by speaking your heart to His presence! Bring your gift, no matter how broken, bring it from the basement, and lay it before Him now!

Part 1 - Chapter 6

THE HOUSE OF THE PRETTY PURPLE DRESS

There is a pretty purple dress in my memory. It was the most beautiful thing I had ever seen. I found it on a special day–my birthday!! I had birthday money in my pocket, and a dress was my only request. My mother took me to the court square in our little town. I remember the bells ringing on the door as we entered the dress shop, and the musty smell of very old buildings on very old town squares.

Inside the dress shop, two women sat behind the counter. I was young, but not too young to soak in the glances that passed between those two women and my mother. I had no idea why everything felt so awkward, but my heart definitely registered that moment as "bad". There were no smiles, no welcome – flatly – no interest. My eagerness won out over the awkwardness, and we cautiously proceeded to the clothing section. I can't help but wonder, now, if those two women baked cakes for their church socials. Did they teach Sunday school? Oh, Heavenly Father, may we never fail to see the precious souls who walk into our days!

My mother found several dresses for me, but I could only shake my head and point again to a deep purple velvet dress hanging on the end. The sleeves were puffed satin – lighter purple – with tiny flowers. It was *beautiful*! I thought it looked like a princess dress! I can remember so well my mom saying, "Well…if you're sure that's the one – okay! We'll take it!"

INSTANTLY those two ladies began to smile and say the sweetest things to us! Almost as instantly I learned something. My heart was snagged. Buy the pretty dresses, and the pretty ladies with the pretty clothes will see you! Every time I put that dress on, I felt so good inside! The new, pretty, purple dress somehow made me visible, and I felt worthy! I felt good! I smiled just walking into my room and seeing it hanging there! The love and attention a mind craves can be drawn from the world with pretty purple dresses!

You see, the House of the Pretty Purple Dress is very bare and very lonely. The only brightness you'll find there will be the dress. And that dress causes people to stop looking past us, and look AT us! The satin and velvet, the fresh smell of new, the bright purple and lavender colors – these things had a special way of comforting in a way few people can understand! The pretty purple dress actually created a little warmth inside! A moment of warmth, a moment of brightness! A moment of "better", as "worse" circled around day after day.

There is an overpowering craving for comfort in some of us. There is an overpowering craving for brightness in all of us. Residents of the House of the Pretty Purple Dress grow up to be precious people spending money they don't have trying to meet needs in one of the only ways they understand! You will find them struggling to buy more and more – struggling to give their children every toy, every game, every "thing" Ralph Lauren, Gap, Tommy Hilfiger, or any other company can dream of to sell them, because truly in their hearts they are trying to give their children warmth and brightness in the only ways they ever found them. It is a habit as addictive and overwhelming as any drug! With credit cards, adult child/parents can be loved all the way up to the limits! And, oh, the sweet relief! – if the love – oops! I mean the limit – runs out – it can be extended; and they can get more!

Unknowing friends greet someone with, "I love those pants," – or, "What a beautiful ring!" – or "nice car." We speak to the belongings rather than the person. Most of the time, we only <u>see</u> the belongs and never <u>see</u> the person! In doing this, a lie is fed, and its effects on a precious soul grow broad and heavy.

So the workdays get longer. Workweeks get longer. A hundred dollars means very little when thousands are needed! The fix lasts shorter periods, and like a drug, the toys get bigger. The price tags grow, and it takes more and more to find the bright rush of comfort!

And we're frantic! Because life without new, pretty, purple dresses would mean no brightness! No comfort! No shiny, new hope!

But dear precious friend, when writing this, I asked myself as well as I'm asking you —

Where is my pretty dress now? Lost somewhere in the attic of my grandmother's old house, I'm sure. The color is faded, no longer bright. The soft, plush velvet is hardened and crumbling with holes. The satin sleeves are crinkled and torn. The comfort it offered lasted a few months.

The brightness it offered could not be sustained; because it was brightness attached to this world!

The world's brightness covers us — brings us out — and people smile at us! The world's brightness goes before us, and we believe it defines who we are! When it fades, we feel we are fading!

THIS IS A TRAP! Prepared by the Father of Lies himself! Satan was the most beautiful, prideful, angelic being created — and I know he and his entire demonic realm thrive on the deception that material brightness is an indicator of the worth of a person! As long as we believe it, we'll chase the material brightness and stay so busy in doing it that we will never know our true worth — our real worth to the ONE waiting outside those heart walls!!

To want brightness may just be something placed in us to draw us to HIM! The reason "bright", "new", "shiny" bring us warmth and comfort is because God Himself is the ultimate of all brightness!!! The brightness of HIS glory will make a person 'as a dead man' — it cannot be looked upon with human eyes! He is splendid, and His brightness never fades! Once again, Satan takes something in a child that God designed for good, and by attaching it to worldly things, twists and distorts it into something unrecognizable when compared to its original intent! Just as Jesus offered the water that would cause us to never thirst again, God's brightness can once and for all satisfy our deepest need for affirmation!

> When we gaze upon Him, and experience HIS light, His brightness begins to warm us, and permeate us — and then go before us! — defining who we are!

His brightness told us of our worth by snuffing out its own

brilliance for three days in order that it might burst forth on the third morning with power and might in order to reach us! Brilliant light animated by warm love!!!

What are your pretty purple dresses, dear friend? Remember those ways we learned to cope as a child as our only means of survival? This is one of them. In part two of this book, I'm going to ask you to leave the House of the Pretty Purple Dress behind – letting go of the bright, shiny things you're collecting there. I hope you'll come with me, out of that house, and move into a house where no appraisals are required. No appraisals on your belongings, no appraisals on your career, or your looks…

You see – the appraisal for your worth was completed a long, long time ago – *on a cross!*

Part 2

INTRODUCTION

The neighborhood we've traveled through has been dark, and for some I know it was difficult. Most of the residents, by nature, are masters of pretending things never happened – masters of disguise – and masters of coping. It's never easy to go back there because it brings awkward, unnerving feelings to the surface. For me, in order to write this book, I had to go back with you so that you could know in your heart that I truly was once your neighbor.

In part two we will look very carefully at how God performed His Banah promise in my house and why man-made methods will never be enough. We will give special attention to how God removes the junk from these forbidden rooms and turns the addictions and losses into independence and strength. I pray that God will prepare the hearts of all who read this for one, true, life changing action. Prayer.

And through your prayers I know God will start tearing down walls and hauling away junk by the soul-load! Making room for the stuff life is made for! God holds it all in heaven to deliver upon demand to all who ask! Pray this prayer now –

Lord,

> I give you complete freedom in my house.
> I'm asking you into
> every corner of every room –
> turn the bright lights on –
> knock down walls –
> haul away the junk –
> blast thru the concrete –
> transform my space in this world.
> Design and create, Lord. I'm ready to move.
> In Jesus Name,

Amen

Part 2 – Chapter 1

"NORMAL" FAÇADE

I want to tell you about a recent dream of mine. The morning after, I could not wait to get to my notebook!

It makes so much sense!

Once again, God was showing me how he brought me to my new house.

I had to get it on paper and get it to you!

In the dream, my husband and I were with some friends in a houseboat on a large lake. The water was rolling and pitching, as it does when a lot of boating activity is going on. Somehow, I fell off the boat and became separated from them. I could see my husband and friends, laughing and talking in the boat, but the water was tossing me. The current was pulling me. As I would shout, the water would enter my mouth and strangle or choke me. I'd go under, and frantically swim and fight, as the turbulent water and the firm undertow continued to pull me farther and farther away! Trying to keep my head above the water and breathe became all that I could do! I fought and swam and fought and swam – and finally found myself in a narrower "channel" of water.

If you've ever gone canoeing, this river type setting is what I'm describing now. Then, do you remember those areas where there are smooth, stone slabs just underneath the surface of water, maybe five or six inches below the surface? You can still feel the rush and the pull of the current, but you can stand on the slab of rock and not be pulled under. After fighting the water for so long to keep from drowning, I pulled up and stood on this kind of smooth stone bottom. It felt so safe!

I was telling myself, "I'll never go to the deep water again! I almost died out there! I'm so tired! It is such relief to stand on this smooth, solid rock bottom!" After a few moments I realized, "Now I can get back to my husband!" I started to walk.

On each side there was brush, thick brush and high hills, tangles of vines. I knew there were snakes. I wanted to cross through those tangles, but I could not! And then I realized I could hear my husband on the other side of the brush! I called him and called him! I cried! I yelled! But, at the same time, I had to keep my eyes on the rock slab or I would miss my step and fall back into the deep current! My husband couldn't hear me! I continued on for a long period of time – hearing my husband on the other side of the tangled vines and thick outgrowth of wild brush – calling and calling out to him – but never taking my eyes off the rock just below the surface! As I moved forward, I gained confidence in the rock and began to run! I was running and splashing through the water – following the path of the rock–hearing my husband and friends on the other side – running to reach them and join them and get back to normal life!

After what seemed like hours and hours of Indiana Jones-type navigation thru this wilderness, by following the path of the rock, I found my way to an opening in the brush. I ran and ran as fast as I could to where my husband was standing with a group of people. But, he was standing with his arm around another lady! He believed I was gone because I wanted to be and had not been trying to get to him, so he had gone on with his life! As my dream ended, he was listening to me – trying to understand where I'd been. If I hadn't awakened and continued to dream, I know how the dream would have ended because I know my husband's heart. He would have gone back with me. I would have shown him the rock. He would have gone back because he believes in me, and he personifies; "live with her in an understanding way."

Now, here's the God connection from my dream…I believe this is a picture of why there is such a high divorce rate, especially among Christians today. My generation, it is full of adult 'child/parents' who have become Christians. We grew up in these other houses, and many of us realized we wanted something different. "Getting in church" sure looks like a step in the right direction! Families in church do say a lot of the right words. They take a lot of the right actions. Many enter into marriage with a sincere, heartfelt desire to commit to the covenant for life. But our normal-looking house is not "true normal". We can hear it and see it in other houses – but we can't get there!

> There is a "normal façade";
> a normal appearance to our home.
> But behind the front,
> behind the face,
> life is not normal.

Eventually, our human strength fails us and we begin to use the child-learned survival techniques. But our ways are not HIS ways. And we begin to slip away – or maybe abruptly fall. The hidden strong undercurrent of the old houses pulls –It will always pull.

It may suddenly and unexpectedly grab and jerk, and the reality is, no attempts with human strength can fight it.

The most perfect husband or wife in the world cannot fight the strength of this undertow. Many give signs of the struggle, but our spouse is busy living, going to work, paying bills, raising children – and they do not understand. The enemy will choke our cry for help with more and more turbulence, more and more pull. As we begin to leave "normal", we can see "normal" still on the boat – but we are absolutely too weakened to come back! And we can't call you because you won't hear us. You who are in the boat love us, and would try to pull us back, but you don't understand what you're pulling against! It's the undertow – the strong undercurrent of the damaged soul! To you, we will seem uncommitted or unpredictable. We may be frigid or cold. We may <u>say</u> one thing and often <u>do</u> another. We're often "sorry" for what we're doing – but then we do it again! We see and hear "normal", but we can't get through to that place!

> Dear friend–who has been blessed to never now
> any house but the "House of Peace and Love,"
>
> Recognize the cry for help of your loves ones!
>
> Rise above the anger at the action or circumstance! Do not give up!

God hates divorce. One reason is because you are the source He would use to lead His drowning child to the Rock in the living fountains of life! They may be drowning – struggling. You may not see or hear them seeking the rock, but rest assure, THEY CAN SEE AND HEAR YOU!! Your strength, your "normal"– is their guide, their pull, their draw to continue following the path of the Rock! God calls and reaches for the lives of His damaged children through you! Thank you so much My Lord for the people you placed in my path to show me true normal!

Though the world might call my husband's patient, peaceful nature weak or boring and apt to be trampled on in a dog-eat-dog world, the God of the universe called it the dynamite power He would use to draw me to Himself! Though the damage be severe, and the world's power ever present, they are not, now, and never will be, stronger than the Godly character traits we, in the deep waters, carefully and continuously observe in you on the boat!

A peace-filled face is always teaching those who are watching.

But back to us–

Dear precious Daddy, Mama, Brother, Sister, Child, Teenager, young adult, and the newly wed,

>Are you drowning? Do you wake up with regret about what happened in your house last night? Do you feel the difference between you and joy? Between you and 'normal'? Do you hear about "normal" and "happy" at church or see it in others – but you cannot get through the tangled vines and brush of what your life has been to where they are? You may be fighting a current of memories, wrong habits, and distorted law of love so strong it is all you can do to keep your head above water and breathe!

>It is so deep! And so cold and dark! The easiest thing for you to do would be to drown!

BANAH

Please read Psalm 61:2 —

> *From the end of the earth will I cry unto Thee, when my heart is overwhelmed, lead me to the Rock that is higher than I.*

From the end of the earth From the darkest rooms of your houses Where the law of love has been broken or is even so distorted it cannot be called "love" anymore From the "ends of the earth"! Yes, beloved, cry from there! (The END means or signifies "the limit" at which a person or "house" ceases to be what they were up to that point -- the point at which previous activities cease!)

I can't persuade anyone to want life to be different, but for those who do, I can promise you there is an end– there is a point where previous activities will stop. Here it is: You must stop swimming.

Here's the picture:

> The overwhelming waters of life which Satan himself
> is the prince or
> ruler of –
> Yourself fighting to survive –
> From the ends of your world you cry –
> GOD, LEAD ME TO THE ROCK! Let me climb onto
> that smooth slab and rest! That smooth, cool slab of rock
> <u>unmoveable</u>! LEAD ME LORD! BRING ME THERE!
> You, God, who are stronger than overwhelming dark waters –
> carry me to that safe Rock!
> Once you cry this out to the Father -- let go.
> *The Power of the Sacrifice has now entered the picture.*
> Let go and let Him.
> Let go of everything you've tried before.

Cling to Him as though he were an air-filled ring! He is the breath of life, beloved!! Hold on as He takes you to the Rock– the Rock peacefully submerged in the trickling, laughing, splashing streams of the waters of life!

And that Rock was Christ.
I Corinthians 10:4

In my dream, when I reached the rock, I rested for a little while. Then I found the strength to stand. Remember, beloved, we've "waxed" strong in the wilderness. The scruples to get up are in there! – In You! – And I began to follow the path of the rock. My goal was life – abundant life– the rock under my feet reassured me the joy was for me too! The Rock is for all! He is not partial!

The pathway will be longer for some of us than others to that place through the clearing where we can finally "partake" of the life we see and hear "over there". Remember, on the cross, Love knew what we must know, and He experienced it to defeat it. In the midst of the sacrifice, the keys to living and dying could no longer exist <u>anywhere</u> but in the nail-scarred hands. They were now only able to exist in Love's power, in Love's purpose for Love's beloved!

In knowledge of the character and life of the Lamb are the keys to *TRUE NORMAL*. As you run through the streams, through the wilderness of emotions to your family and friends on the other or "normal"side, you will still feel the flow – the undercurrent – pulling against you! There will be dangerous crevices and drop-offs where the dark waters rush. Take your eyes off the Rock and you will fall! Weaknesses and injury from time spent in the deep waters before may cause you to slip off, or trip and fall! But, dear friend, the *ROCK WON'T MOVE*! Once you've found Him, you've found Him! Grab hold, again,

    find your strength,

        and climb back on!!!

There on the Rock, you must come to *know* the Rock intimately.. Conforming to the solid character of the Rock is the key to true normal!

Learn of His character. Learn of his ideas about life and

temperament, house rules and love rules! He faced all evil. Its greatest sting dissolved before Him! You follow the path of the Rock as you learn of Him. One step at a time, gently, He will reveal to you what must be let go of – to be replaced by something of His knowledge. By conforming to His likeness – choosing to respond to every situation as He would – you will defeat your weakness! The tangled vines and thick brush will begin to thin and fall away. You'll then stand in the clearing, ready to really live among your loved ones. The solid strength of the Rock will be inside of you – unshakable! You'll be able to commit to commit to your family and give to them the gifts the Rock has produced in your life. And, praise God, for the first time in your life, you can receive their love without fear!!

> He is the Rock, His work is perfect– for all
> His ways are judgment.
> A God of truth and without iniquity,
> just and right is He!
> And once again,
> Praise the King!
> Who Is, and Was, and Is to Come!
> Praise Him for His plan!
> Praise Him for His provisions!
> Praise Him for His Peace!
> Praise Him, for you will reach true normal!

Part 2 – Chapter 2

A DISSERTATION ON CLOGGED PLUMBING

Living in a house void of warmth and love causes something inside of us that I've labeled clogged plumbing. Years of holding feelings inside, especially warm love, changed our ability to have a natural flow occur. When young, we held it back for a reason. -- When older, we *can't* let it flow. Warmth and love are stuck at a lump right in the center of our chest! Randomly, small amounts may leak around that lump, and frequently, in the case of our own children, somewhat of a steady, sputtering stream may flow through, but it carries pieces of debris. Debris that touches our childrens' lives and leaves its mark. I wrote the following lines about love trying to describe the healing that has taken place in me. Psalm 19:7 says, *"The testimony of the Lord is sure."* As God has unclogged my plumbing and opened up my chest, I know it is a testimony about who He is and how He loves. My whole life is a testimony to His goodness!

> *The pipes in this chest swell and almost burst when I think of Him!! And the love that pours out of me now gushes freely! Endlessly!*
> *Warmly!*

Please, dear friend, read on…

God's Love

> *Long ago and far away from our houses, God looked down upon the earth and saw the clay of men and women crumbling.*
>
> *But God is love. Love that saves everything it touches. Knowing this, God moved toward the clay and prepared to provide a way to infuse the crumbling clay with the love of God. Love, filling*
>
> *Heaven through and through, spilled over out of Heaven and down onto the earth and wrapped Himself in the crumbling clay.*

Oh, how the warm love must have shone through the eyes and voice of this clay that became His vessel to reach us!

And then one day, Love spilled over, out of that clay, and onto the ground below. As the Love touched the earth, the way was made forever for Love to infuse all clay, to restore all clay, to save all clay from crumbling!

Love would infuse the clay with new life and enable the time spent on earth to be spent in the flowing warmth of Him! No more crumbling now. The flow moistens the clay – causing it to adhere and hold form. The day Love was spilled out onto the earth, the clay that housed it crumbled. But Heaven's Love was <u>never</u> <u>determined</u> by the frailty of the clay. Love resurrected the clay and in doing so demonstrated His ability to give life to the crumbled clay of all by infusing the love of Heaven directly into it.

Love spilled over –
To be part of us!
To infuse us –
And enable us to love.
For clay was made to love and be loved forever.
God moved first. He came to us. In Him there is no turning, no fear, and no weakness.

In Him is steady, flowing, warm love, deep and penetrating, able to infuse our hearts and minds, opening our chest, opening the flow that was clogged so long ago, allowing us to feel, wanting us to feel, love. Free and warm.
Forever.

Pour your love into Him. Ask Him in prayer to cause you to love Him more and more and you will feel the infusing of His warmth open your chest wide!

And before you know it, love not hindered by the frailty of your clay will be pouring out of you!! It will be mingled with His love and it will bathe your family, your friends, and your world in its warmth! It will wash over everyone who enters the room you're in! You see, He's still using the clay to deliver His love to the earth! This testimony is sure! How God loves! The sureness of His love will never be described completely with our words! But the infusing of the clay, the opening of the chest, *this is* a testimony that walks and talks and gives abundant life to all who come near!

No, precious friend, your plumbing can't be clogged in the new house! God's Love invited and infused into the life of a believer dissolves the lump of suffering affection. The desire to love when love is not received is forever removed, for the clay, and for the Loving Savior. It is replaced by a lifetime of pure flowing warmth between you and Love Himself, and out of you into the world around you.

Praise Him now– For God is Love.

Part 2 – Chapter 3

BEAMS OF SECURITY ON FOUNDATIONS OF PEACE

In the "House of Fear," many of you understood the language of tears deep in the night when other houses were asleep. You can feel it as well as if it were yesterday – the suffering affection for the beloved cowering underneath the fear that covered us as tangibly as the blankets we kept pulled up to our noses. We were often stilled by fear, immobilized, and knew full well we were powerless to stop what was happening. We grew accustomed to lying or standing rigid in its grip. We skipped the introduction in life to peace and security, but we never knew it. You don't miss things you've never known. Please let me introduce you today to a house stabilized by strong beams of security laid on a foundation of peace.

Many people who missed the early introduction find it difficult to move into a house of peace. Accustomed to fear and turmoil, stable and quiet is often rejected as dull and boring, but the real truth is, when things get quiet and peaceful, we don't know what to do with ourselves. Our stance has been poised, on guard, rigid for so long, that, to be quiet and peaceful is in itself frightening! We know how to react to fear, or better yet, we've learned how to function in its grip. And this known house with its rigid poise feels safer than an unknown house! To move about in life with guarded rigidity makes us feel clumsy in the House of Peace! Not unlike a 'bull in a china shop' sort of way! Even though I understand how you feel – here's the bottom line:

> *God has not given us a spirit of fear, but of power, love, and a sound mind.*
>
> *2 Timothy 1:7*

Now, look closely at the spirit of a sound mind as opposed to a spirit of fear. *"God has not given us the spirit"* – the spirit is that thing in a person by which we perceive, think, and feel. God's infusing of Himself in us causes us not to perceive, think, and feel from a rigid stance of fear, but, instead we will perceive, think, and feel from a "sound" mind. The original Greek word for "sound" was "sophros". This literally means "safe". Safe, whole, and healthy. Safe what? Mind– that part of us that feels, makes judgment calls, and determines our next move every minute of the day. The part that was damaged deep in the night!

God's renewing touch replaces fear with serene security. We begin to react to life from a stance of complete safety! Remember, fear causes a "casting down from a sense of security". Making decisions and responding to life from the rigid spirit of fear causes misjudgments, missed opportunities, and misconceptions of the good intentions of good people.

Responding to life and making your decisions from solid and serene security, from a sound mind, causes skillful, wise judgment calls, seized and realized opportunities, and easy, trusting relationships with good people!

A spirit that responds out of safety and security, rather than fear, rests on a foundation that finds its strength in quiet peace. The word <u>peace</u> means easy, quiet, and harmonized relationships between you and the people around you, and between you and God. It involves friendliness, and it makes your life "whole" and "full". The word "whole" is used in the Greek almost interchangeably with "healthy" and "sound". These are the promised effects of what God gives His child. But change <u>will never</u> occur apart from being in His presence! Reading this book or talking with pastors, counselors, and therapists will not heal your spirit from the effects of the house of fear. But bending your knees and bowing your head and opening the doors of your heart and mind before the Lord will! It will make you a different person. People will ask you how you do it – and all you'll be able to say is, "It's Him!" Every moment in His presence allows Him to place strong beams of security on your sorely needed foundation of peace!

From the testimony of many individuals who lived in the house of fear, I have found that some of the most common baggage we've carried into adulthood is "yelling". Yelling at spouse and yelling at children. For the Christian, this brings deep feelings of guilt and shame. But, praise God, condemnation does not come from Him! In Christ there is no condemnation. In Christ we can be healed! Whole! Sound! and responding to our loved ones from a quiet peace within! The wrath of man does not ever produce the righteousness of God! All of our yelling is simply recreating the same casting down from a sense of security in our children that we experienced, and breeds more wrong reactions and wrong responses in them! It causes them to rebel more!

When God begins to place the beams of security on foundations of peace in our houses, it breaks terrible generational patterns in our families! Gone is the grip of fear, gone is the loudness, the falling. No more sense of loss of control—only peace. Soft, quiet, and predictable. Letting your rigid guard down is no longer frightening because it's unfamiliar and not trusted, but a welcomed, relaxed position from which to live your life. Welcome, my friend! Welcome to this neighborhood!

I want to tell you about a day when my first daughter was very small. My dear husband was working in another part of the house and overheard me yelling at my precious little girl. Remember, our nature is to repeat the patterns we've known, and this is "normal" to someone who's never lived in a house of peace. God has gifted my husband with the most awesome ability to live with me in an understanding way! He came and found me. Very quietly he said, "Could you come with me for a minute?" I followed him and he led me into a small bathroom at the back of the house. He closed the door, turned to me, and as he leaned down over me, he yelled at the top of his lungs, **"DO YOU REMEMBER HOW IT FEELS!?!"**

It shook me to my bones. Immediately, I began to cry hot, bitter tears of shame. Because when he yelled at me, my insides cringed and collapsed into the memories he had awakened.

But he then wrapped warm and understanding arms around me, holding me carefully as I cried, and gave me back my dignity!

Somehow, this man knew what to do to teach me through trust! He just says he prayed for wisdom. Go figure! Since then, together, with our children, we humble ourselves before one another and ask for forgiveness <u>if</u> the yelling occurs. Through truth and self humbling, God gives the grace needed to stop the generational patterns of verbal abuse. The damage increases when there is lack of parent control.

You may not have a spouse capable of this kind of compassion, but you have a Father in Heaven who's capable of this and more! He'll wrap warm arms of love around you and, as He reveals your mistakes to you, He will change you! You collapse into shame but He gives you dignity! You can <u>trust</u> His life-giving remodeling of your soul!

There's one more part of this change that needs to be discussed. I see my mom and dad through God's eyes. What happened to me had happened to them years before, and worse. God enabled me to understand this in such a way that compassion drowns out all bitterness. I also understand that my grandparents probably were child parents who learned to live in a house of fear as well. Remember, it's generational layers!

Bitterness and unforgiveness will hold your beams of fear securely in place. <u>Only</u> God can demolish beams of fear. The fusion of his love dissolves the bitterness and unforgiveness. He then applies a cement mixture of compassion and forgiveness to your foundation in which He sets the new Beams of Security on that solid foundation of peace down deep in your soul. The foundation of peace is that mixture of forgiveness and compassion. There can never be a foundation of peace without them. As all of this construction is taking place, your spirit of fear is steadily replaced by a sound, whole, healthy spirit that will move and will respond to every person and every circumstance around you with quietness and gentleness that can be explained by no other means but thy Lord, the Lord, and thy God, that pleadeth the cause of His people, has done a <u>good</u> thing in you!

Pray this prayer, NOW!

BANAH

Lord Jesus,

You have not given me a spirit of fear – the
houses of fear robbed me and my family of any
sense of security in this world. As a result, often
there is no peace in my house, even today. But Lord,
you promise in your Word that you give your child
a spirit of power, love, and a sound mind. I want
to claim what you've promised me today – this day!
I'm looking to you, my creator, my Father, the Holy
One who gives me life to place in me strong beams
of security on a foundation of peace, a peace made up
of compassion and forgiveness. I trust your goodness.
I want my mind to know "safety". I want to respond
to life from a whole and healthy spirit. I want to shine
with a quiet and gentle peace.
I ask you to begin this work in me today.
Thank you.
I love you.

Amen

    The father loves you, dear friend! And so do I!

Part 2 – Chapter 4

THE LAMP IN THE DEN

My husband and I have an ongoing battle in our house. I turn lamps on – He turns them off! I'm serious! I have a thing about lamps! I come home and turn lamps on, usually in every room. For a long time, my husband would be so aggravated, thinking I was being forgetful and leaving them on for no reason! I want to try and explain to you my love for these lamps.

I always wanted to belong to my family. I'm not ashamed to say it! I wanted to come home after school and at night to my mother and my father – not my grandparents – not my step-family's, though they were precious to me, - but MY mom and MY dad. I wanted to see them sitting together on a couch in a den with a lamp on -- waiting for me. That was my secret picture! In my mind's eye, all through the years, telling the world that I didn't want it at all – I must confess now that my heart wanted it more than anything! My secret picture always had a warm glow – the lamp – shining softly through the window – through the doorway.

Will you believe me if I tell you, moms and dads, that even if your house has aunts, uncles, grandparents, brothers, or sisters at home, your child is still experiencing "The Empty House" if <u>YOU</u> are not there? I realize it is not logical to believe you could be there <u>every</u> day – but often – please – try for "often". Make sure you're there waiting for them -- and turn on a lamp!

My lamps welcome my children home! My heart reads a lamp in the den as a symbol of expectancy! House after house after house will never be a home – because the little people do not know the warmth of someone eagerly awaiting their arrival -- looking to see their face come through the door– and knowing no other face will fill the expecting heart but their own! When I'm turning on lamps, I'm calling them in!
I'm saying,
    "Here I am!

Looking for you – and you alone!
Welcome home my precious ones!
Rest from your day!
Let me love you until you have to go back out into the world tomorrow!"

This is what makes coming into a house coming "home"!

I found a really cool thing in the scriptures. Revelations 4:5 says something remarkable:

In Heaven, my Father sits on a throne......
and there are **seven lamps** burning around Him!
Seven, perfect and complete lamps!
WOW!

When I told my husband, he said, "I guess you think I'd be going around trying to turn those off too!" Then he said, "Nah, I won't have to pay the power bill there!"

Do you realize what I'm saying to you, my fellow empty-house alumni? He's waiting up for us! Eagerly, expectantly waiting for us to come home! He doesn't sleep! He does not slumber! The lamps will never be turned off! And Heaven won't be empty!

My whole life, as I pictured that one lamp in the den, I had no idea my Father had SEVEN! Now my secret picture is a throne instead of a couch! And the room is ablaze with seven beautiful lamps! He's saying,

"Welcome!
I'm looking so forward to seeing your face!
Come in and let me love you!
Rest from your days!
Just be with me as I am with you!"

I said "My Father" has seven lamps...

"My Father" – how wonderful it feels to say that! MY FATHER! Years ago, during the weeks before Father's day, I didn't listen to Christian radio talk shows. Though I usually love Christian Radio, this time of year clouded my mind and brought a familiar ache to my chest. I have always longed to have a close relationship with my dad. – If given the chance, I think I would have been a "daddy's girl"! Each year I would try to find some kind of Father's Day card to send him. This task brought me low, because they all said so many things that just weren't a part of our life together. So I turned off the radio, stopped trying to look through the greeting cards, and just withdrew into dread of the church service that would lay open my wound once again. Not only could I not honor him because he wasn't there, the praise of all the other fathers brought attention to my father's absence – the absence a daughter's heart still longed to cover and defend! I still would today, by the way. God loves my father. I will never stop praying for the Banah promise to be performed in his life, too! And, at that time, I would love to be a part of it! Now let me tell you the wonderful part of this story! One year, about the time of Father's Day, I was sitting in the recliner in my den. It was 11 p.m. I had been reading, but had closed my book, and the ache started way down deep in my chest. I asked God, "Why?" Why couldn't I have a life with my dad? I wanted to love one everyday! I wanted one to love me every day! There was a precious coach who taught my sixth grade class in school – I remember pretending I was his child! He was so kind! Then there was a wonderful local grocer who hired me after school during my teen years. He was patient and strong, and offered wisdom and understanding, many times when he had <u>no idea</u> of the void he was filling! Please, Christian friends, hear me when I promise you, the kindness you offer to young people in these houses will not go unrewarded! The Bible story of planting seeds – especially in the fertile ground of a child – is true! So true! I wish they all could see my house today!

That night in my den, as I asked God the why's, He did something I'm now very familiar with. He gave no clear answer – He simply fixed the problem. The Spirit of God spoke to my heart and said, "I'm your daddy". At this point in my life, I had not found the "Father of the Fatherless" scriptures – but the Word came alive in my heart that night. The hole in my chest was filled – the balm of Gilead I think they call it – was applied to the wound and closed it forever. It has never hurt me since that night, and I feel no sense of loss. I'm concerned for the well-being of my earthly father – spiritually and physically. I will always do everything he allows me to in order to help him. I will always love him from a distance, not by choice; but because he keeps me there.

But when God said, "I'm your daddy" – He immediately began to teach and train me in all of the ways of life my earthly father could not. And I've never since felt the need to substitute other godly men in my life for a dad – the need is met. Once and for all. A done deal. Healed and free, in a moment, between me and Him!

Boy, was this a sappy sight! A fully grown young woman realizing she could climb into her dad's lap for the very first time! I know when I get to heaven, I'll be down on my face for quite a while – even now His presence is so "felt" at times I feel like I should crawl instead of walk! But as soon as this "self" realizes it's changed – and able to stand – I'm going straight to His lap! That's my goal! I'm gonna climb right up in the middle of all those lamps and tell Him about my day!

I've heard many mothers cry for their children, and they're saying through the tears, "but he doesn't have a daddy!" YES, HE DOES! He has a father who will raise him to stand before heaven in strength and wholeness! And with more excellence than any earthly father could attempt! You tell your child, mothers! Don't let them hurt another day! Tell them God said, "I'm your daddy!" Then hit your knees and start praying for the Banah promise in their earthly daddy's life!

And someday, if I ever find the means, I plan to do something about those greeting card sections on Father's Day and on Mother's Day! There'll be a whole section of cards to purchase that speak of love, forgiveness, and hope for the future to our earthly parent, a whole section speaking thanks and gratitude to those who stepped in during our lives, and a section especially written to inspire worship of our Father! We can buy this card, and send it with our message of hope to the fatherless around us! And at church, when everyone else stands up and tells of a loving relationship with their father – we'll stand up and tell of our own! Now days, instead of dread or "pretending it's not happening", I really look forward to the day of the year set aside to honor my Father! The one who placed seven lamps around the chair where He's waiting for me.

The world may not understand it, but I am loving my family when I turn the lamps on! As the warm love of my Father unclogged my plumbing, and gave me a façade of true normal, beams of security, and a foundation of peace, He <u>enabled</u> me to love so completely! When infused with His love and His spirit, I received wisdom and understanding, counsel and might, knowledge and fear of the Lord! My heavenly Father imparted to me the character traits my earthly father could not! He enabled me to fill an empty house with warm lamplight and make it a home! In my old house, I would have never grasped true normal and, behind the false façade, I would never have turned the first lamp on! My children would have lived their young lives in an empty house – alone and afraid – looking and wishing for that lamp when they came home each day! I can't go on without praying!

Thank you, Father!

You planted love <u>in</u> me <u>for</u> my
family that is like <u>your</u> love <u>for</u> me! As you wait on
the throne for me to come home, you're allowing me to
eagerly wait in my house every day for them to come
home to me! What a gift! Thank you! Thank you for
this richness of life! And thank you for turning the
lamp on in me!

Love always,
Your Child

If you live in an empty house, you just remember – your Father sits waiting for you with seven lamps brightly burning. If you have children, you should surprise them <u>often</u> and you should be there when they come home and remember to turn your lamp on! The lamp in your den, and the lamp in your heart!

> *After this I looked, and, behold, a door was opened in heaven: and the first voice which I heard was as it were of a trumpet talking with me, which said, "Come up hither, and I will show thee things which must be hereafter." And immediately, I was in the spirit: and, behold, a throne was set in heaven, and One sat on the throne – and out of the throne proceeded lightning and thundering and voices: and there were seven lamps of fire burning before the throne...*
>
> *Revelations 4: 5*

WOW!

Part 2 – Chapter 5

CALL SANFORD AND SON!

Fred and Lamont Sanford owned a junkyard in prime-time TV land most of my young life. Every episode began with the theme song as they drove that broken-down old truck through town with the junk they picked up for the day. I couldn't help but think of them as I thought about how to deal with the House of the Forbidden Room. The house where drugs are used, manufactured, sold -- it doesn't matter which -- in your life, it's time that it all is confronted, labeled, and hauled to the junkyard.

First, it's true that you can pocket more money in one day selling drugs than in two weeks of hard labor in a local factory. But, it's also true that *"wealth gotten by vanity SHALL be"* diminished, but he that *"gathereth by labor SHALL increase." (Proverbs 13:11)*. Now look, we've learned a lot in this book about how much God loves us. He didn't say in this verse that the person's wealth would increase. He said the <u>person</u> would!

Dear Friend, I'm convinced that if money could make us happy, God would have it grow on the trees instead of leaves! But labor seems to be an important part of making us better men and women. In one way, our fallen nature is learning to stand up again through an honest day's work! God has said,

> Better is little with the respect of the things of God in your house than great treasure and the trouble that comes with it.

Proverbs 15:16

And He said,
> *He that tilleth his land shall be 'satisfied' with bread.*

Proverbs 28:19

You may have more money in the House of the Forbidden Room, but you will never be "satisfied" with all the things in the world it might buy! Moral riches are possessed by God, not for sale. Moral riches are offered freely.

Many times in the Bible the word "piece" is used for money, "piece of silver". "Piece," means, "that which should fill." But it doesn't and it never will! Not like the "peace" of being morally right before God! Go figure!

Second, you may be a user. I won't argue against the powerful effects of a drug. I won't argue the escape it may provide you from pain or disillusionment with the life you've been handed by your own "parent/children". I won't even argue the fact that in the beginning, using was fun and brought its two best friends with it -- popularity and attention. I won't argue these things -- but I will <u>beg</u> you to open your eyes and see the end of the story!

See the little eyes who see you! Little eyes filled with suffering affection. And your Father's eyes of suffering affection. They suffer because they see you fading– the fading brilliance of your life falling from the highs, the side effects, the after effects, the tremors, and the moods.

And I will beg you to remember the Power of the Sacrifice -- to remember that no grip of addiction exists that this Power cannot break!

> *Love the Lord your God with <u>all your heart!</u> Lean not into your own understanding! But in <u>every</u> minute – in <u>all</u> your ways – look to Him!*
>
> *Proverbs 3:5*

Ask for the Power of the Sacrifice to blast through your chains and release you from addiction! Claim the Power in prayer before the Father every day!

As a child, I remember leaning my head back and singing "Bobby McGee" at the top of my lungs – Janis Joplin's anthem of freedom would seem to have been our family's theme song. Everything from the "dirty red bandana" and "feeling faded as my jeans" to listening to "Bobby sing the blues" was our way of life. The only peaceful memory in my mind of my parents is one of my mother sitting alongside my dad as he played the guitar and sang. She harmonized with him, and this is how we passed the time. I pulled out my Janis Joplin tape and listened again as I was writing this book. Oh, how the memories flowed! But as usual, God began to speak to my heart with His sweet words of truth, and He took me to a place in His word I wish my loved ones could have understood all those years ago – Galations 5.

I believe the words used in the song – writings of a generation reflect their perception of life, of their circumstances, and of how to live in those circumstances. In light of that fact, take a deeper look at this song...

> *Freedom's just another word for nothing left to lose. Nothing don't mean nothing if it ain't free. Feeling good was easy, Lord, when Bobby sang the blues. Feeling good was good enough for me. Good enough for me and my Bobby McGee.*

Freedom is a release from restraint or obligation. Now what do you suppose this generation wanted a release from? I understand rebellion against God's law in order to fulfill the lust of the flesh, but that's not what I'm talking about here. I believe many of these people were disillusioned by what had happened in their own houses. Many of their father's had come home from World War II as completely different men. These men had never known anything but raising a family and making a home. They had been called away to the killing fields of war, and bravely faced the call to defend our freedom. These young men were as unfamiliar with killing as you or I would be, and war left its mark. The fathers were hardened, shocked, and different. The mothers were alone. They lived daily wondering if their husbands were dead or alive. Raising children with little money, little support, and little comfort. Many parents of our parents turned to alcohol for relief. These became our first communities of houses void of warmth and love – and our house with the forbidden room had a forerunner – the house with the forbidden cabinet.

They longed to feel good. They longed for ease. They longed to forget the horrors of war and the loneliness of separation. Addictions eased them.

Their inability to explain this to their children caused their children – our parents – to follow a spin-off of what they saw at home. And freedom to our parents became – "just another word for nothin' left to lose." If you threw off all restraint and obligation, you certainly had nothing left to lose! And feeling good <u>is</u> good enough when you're not obligated – and not restrained – by family, or children, or the law.

But family, and children, and the law remain. They don't cease to exist because the highs seem to release us from obligation to them. Feeling good is not good enough when we take a sober look at the truth. Throwing off restraint doesn't throw these people away. And the pain is multiplied ten-fold when we look first at a war-torn family and then watch with shocked disbelief the CNN headline news alerts today. Remember, the thief always takes God's truth and gives us a counterfeit that destroys us.

True freedom is <u>not</u> "just another word for nothing left to lose". With true freedom, my dear precious friends, you have everything to gain. Individually, I cannot visit each and every place you the reader may have been. But there is <u>one</u> individual <u>freedom</u> for each and every one of us. The release the addictions seem to provide is offered freely in the sacrifice.

Would you agree with me that "death annuls all obligations"? Jesus, the sacrifice of God's life, annuls all restraints on our lives. This freedom's just another word for gaining control of your life. Full, rich, abundant life. **How**? When you're addicted to crystal meth or 100 proof Vodka, **How**?

Galations 5:
> *Stand fast therefore in the freedom*
> *wherewith Christ hath made us free...*
> *Remember standing on the Rock?*
> *We must stand on this knowledge of the truth about Jesus!*

Through the Spirit, we have the hope of freedom , by faith in Jesus' sacrifice.

Galations 5: 5 & 6
> *For we through the Spirit wait for the*
> *hope of righteousness by faith.*
> *For in Jesus, neither circumcision nor*
> *uncircumcision availeth anything –*
> *But faith which worketh by love.*

The "freedom" wherewith the sacrifice has made us <u>free</u> releases us from the <u>restraint</u> of the addiction. What we have done, right or wrong, high or sober, has availed nothing in our lives. Our hope is in what His love animated by brilliant light in us can do.

Faith in Jesus works <u>by</u> love. (Galations 5:6) Remember how the Love of Heaven spills out and fuses with the clay? (See Part 2, Chapter 2 "Clogged Plumbing"). The Love fusing with the clay moistens it and causes it to adhere together, take form, and be molded into something new. Faith in Jesus, making us new by the fusing of Love in our clay, works in us to free us from the desire for the drug. Please understand me! Your body may lust for the drug. Your mind may feel the restraint of the past. But the Holy Spirit can fuse you together and release you from all restraints when your faith and your hope is placed in the sacrifice!

In the Old Testament, we are told many times how the temple sacrifices were made before the cross.

> *And thou shalt prepare a meat offering for it*
> *every morning, the sixth part of an ephah, and*

the third part of a hin of <u>oil</u>, to <u>temper</u> with <u>the</u>
<u>fine flour</u> –
                                              Ezekiel 46:14

    The oil represents the Holy Spirit, Who was released to us through the Cross. To "temper" means "to mix with". It is to mix in such a way as we learned in high school chemistry – two separate substances joined together to form a compound. The properties change in such a way that the compound can never be separated again– it is a new substance. It cannot go back to the way it once was. The flour is the clay. Unleavened clay is Jesus– perfect and unmixed. Leavened clay would be us–mixed with things that make us unperfect and blemished. We need the oil to change us, cause us to take a new form, hold shape, and be new.

    Through the Sacrifice, the Holy Spirit can enter and fuse with the clay – temper it – and change it into something new and different. Just as the oil tempers the fine flour in Ezekiel 46. And remember, to temper means a new substance is formed that cannot be separated back into oil and flour. Once the Holy Spirit has tempered the clay, the change is real, it is thorough, the very properties of your nature have changed, and it cannot ever be undone. If mistakes overwhelm certain areas of your life, you may need to temper your clay with more of the precious oil of gladness, the oil of faith, the oil of the God's spirit working in you! Request it, beloved! Ask, and He delights to give!.

    The restraint of the drug was crucified in the sacrifice. Obligation to it annulled. The restraint of addiction died on the cross. We are given a new spirit by which to live when we cast all dependence upon the One who overcame. The fruit, the natural effect, or result of that new spirit is "temperance".

Galations 5: 22 & 23
But the fruit of the spirit is love, joy, peace,
longsuffering, gentleness, goodness, faith,
meekness, <u>temperance</u>; against such there

is no law.

Temperance means strength – strong self control.
Temperance equals Power bestowed by God on you for your will to be operated by the Spirit of God! Hallelujuh! Praise Him for His provision!

Do you understand? Oil-filled clay equals strong self-control. Spirit-filled equals self-control. You receive God-given power to allow your will – whether or not to use the drug – to be operated by the Holy Spirit. And you are left free to gain. And now when you feel good, the high won't be followed by a crash. This freedom is free. You stop spending grocery money to buy the high. Once again, simply get on your knees, tell Him of your need, allow the fusion of His love in you to take place, and <u>stand</u> in the power of the Sacrifice!

Freedom's just another word for everything to gain.
Everything means everything, and it's free.
Feelin' good is easy, Lord, when we're really free…
Feelin' good is good enough for me…
Good enough for me and <u>my</u>…

You get the picture.

There is a plan and a provision to free us from addiction. Faith in His Love fusing in our house. We gain our health, our peace, and our family. Seeking release from pain and confusion, many threw off responsibility thinking they were throwing off restraint. Only to find themselves restrained by a thief waiting to destroy them and their loved ones. If you live here, walk away from this house, beloved. Throw away the bottle. Load up the junk. Let's haul. You don't need it anymore.

Thirdly, you may not sell or use, but you may deeply love those who do.

It's true, there will be no forbidden room in your new house. Nothing is salvageable from this one. Piece by piece, all wood, brick, and mortar that's left must be hauled away. That's why I thought of Sanford and Son– it's all junk that's got to go so we'll be needing the truck! People may notice when we come thru town! But, if we don't haul this junk away, leaving the counterfeit riches, counterfeit popularity, and false highs in the junk pile, then those you love may never know <u>real</u> love at all! After junking the junk, you will have the opportunity to invite them to your new house! And like Habitat for Humanity– you can help them raise a new house of their own! It's true, when you first start moving, the beloved may criticize and ostracize! They don't have a clue that your new house could be only the first in your family's whole community of new houses! Faithful is He that calleth you, who also will do it! Please trust God and know that **you may be the only way those in your house will ever know God's love**! It *won't* be easy, but it *will* be worth it! If just one– one of them stops the fall from the high and finds the truth! Oh, what joy!

Believe me, I know that to see your loved one get a new house brings <u>more</u> joy than even living in one of your own! My sister's house is now filled with warm love, too!

So now, very carefully, let's pull the truck around and back it up to the door– load it up– "level-full" (that's Southern!) play the Sanford and Son theme song in your head– and haul it away. Turn your back on that which will drain your very life from you.

With God as my witness, I fear nothing that He calls me to. His power goes before me, His strength is underneath me like the wind, and His might my rear-guard. His grace covers my head, and His beauty surrounds me! Loved ones lost when I moved out were already lost to the addictions long before I left. Loved ones who climbed in the truck and helped me haul are no longer fading away, but living rich, brilliant lives.

To really reach those you deeply love, start hauling away the junk.
        Clean out the forbidden.
                Dump the illegal.
Learn of the intoxicating high we get from the precious Holy Spirit!

Learn to sell this high to the people around you. Reap the riches of life in ways you've never imagined!! Trade your "pieces" for peace!

Fred Sanford used to clutch his heart and shout, "Elizabeth, I'm comin' to join you, Honey!" He spent his life hauling away junk, and looked forward to going "up yonder" with his beloved wife. To me, this is the good life– to help people haul away their junk and look forward to heaven. I hope in some way that's what this book does for you – help you get rid of your junk and want heaven. If it does, my heart's prayer has been answered.

Part 2 – Chapter 6

WINDOWS TO THE SOUL

I'm finding it very difficult to address the effects of pornography in a home for the great fear of somehow giving advertisement to the it! -- Or in some way triggering imagery in the mind of the reader as we plow through this. That's just what I intend to do – plow through it! – For I detest this house above all! But the gift is so broken for many that even carefully written, well intended, Christian material can send them spiraling down, down, down into torrents of raging mind wars! The occupants of this house are so vulnerable! The mildest references are kegs of dynamite!

The saddest thing is that the Christian who wants to leave this house is almost always trying to do it alone. You and I will never know how many fellow Christians hide there. These dear people know no other life but perpetual secrecy!

I want to make a promise to all of you with a broken gift. I promise you today that your beams of security on a foundation of peace with its true normal façade will have very beautiful details – for example – new windows.

Windows.

New windows.

Looking out the windows each morning, usually we'll make our decision about what to wear that day. Bright sunshine will bring us cheer – gray skies and rain bring us gloom. Light shining through makes our house warm and bright, and we move quickly away when lightning flashes and the wind howls. In cities like New Orleans, there are wrought iron bars over the windows due to the high crime rate of the area. Those windows are an entryway into the house that must be fortified – wrought iron protection to keep that which would do harm from entering in.

Dear precious friend, the eyes are the windows to your soul. Those things that entered our tiny windows as children entered like a thief and went straight to the basement to hide! Day after day, week after week, the thief who comes to steal, kill, and destroy entered and worked feverishly to prepare the network of traps and land mines and pits to use for the theft of our purity, the destruction of truth, and the killing of love that is right and whole and good at the first opportunity afforded!

I ran into someone who lived in my house of the broken gift recently. I felt the gaze from their windows size me up – and they then left the window. Though their countenance was facing me – "they" left the window. They never got past my physical appearance to my windows. If they had, they would have found me gazing through at them with warmth and love. As I walked away from the quick, superficial, and awkward meeting, I felt so bad for this person. The thief took our relationship away many years ago. Not just this person's relationship with me, but this person's relationship with everyone in our house. Years of addiction to pornography – the proven, documentable personality and life changes that it brings about – means there are no bonds there between us. These people don't see the windows in their family. They see the product of the thief in their mind's eye, and substitute that for the eyes of the people in their house. If the product of the thief has stopped you from looking out your windows into the windows of your loved ones, and instead has you gazing through the window of your mind's eye and looking at false windows that display things that exalt themselves against the sovereign purity and goodness of God, then you, dear one, are being robbed blind of the depth and richness offered to you in this life. The relationships with your spouse and children and grandchildren are being killed – insidious and grotesque murders of the heart and soul – and the golden warmth of the seasons of your life ultimately and completely destroyed.

So what do we do with a house when this thief has already entered and set up residence? The chief tool he uses against us is the video template he plays at will in our mind's eye. Even when convinced to fortify our windows and prevent the thief from entering anymore – the images have been "engraved" onto that plate and can be played at will of you or the thief.

As I said before, I intend to plow through this house, not one image can be left on that template! The Bible relates "plow" to "engraving". Listen.

> *The sin of Judah is written with a pen of iron, and with the point of a diamond: it is graven upon the table of their heart..."*
> *Jeremiah 17:1*

Even though we were children when the thief started slipping through our windows, the sin was sin – and child or not – the engraving occurred. It had a mind of its own, a mind set to steal, kill, and destroy. A mind set to distort, twist, and misuse the gift!

So what we must do, dear friend, is place that pen of iron with the sharp point of a diamond in the hand of God and ask Him to "plow" through the sin that has been engraved in our soul! Do you understand? Those images will be engraved in us until the Master Artificer plows through the plate! The *worst* thing you can do is continue to live in secrecy before your Master Artificer! The diamond pointed pen of iron must be applied to the stuff engraved in our mind's eye – and allowed to plow through and through by His skilled and precise hand!!

You may manage to stop the outward infiltration of your windows, but you do not have the diamond point to plow your brain! Only God. Only God. You may never let another soul on earth know what has entered your windows, or how terribly broken your gift actually was. But I'm asking you, how badly do you want a new house? You have no choice but to let the Master Artificer in. You release your faith into action of the pen when you speak your secrets to Him! He loves you. The whole of His justice and His Holiness will consume sin and melt it like wax. He can't be part of who He is. You speak to the countenance of the suffering Savior with passion in His eyes for you, and you can *trust* Him to deal with the sin in a complete and just way. He'll plow through and redesign your gift into its intended perfection.

Prayer, my friend. Speaking the secrets and requesting the pen of the Master plow through the engravings on your heart and soul. Then your new house with new windows will be fortified within and without.

Without.

Speaking of without, I came across an article in the October 2002 issue of <u>Redbook</u> listing the following statistics: Of the people polled, 78% said they are concerned about what their children see on TV, 67% are concerned about the amount of sexual content on TV, and 69% believe sexual content is increasing. 63% said the TV screen is obscene and 59% said they're "concerned" about what shows like "The Osbournes" say about family life.

I'm *SCREAMING– Why is this not 100%!?* Where are the former residents of this house when these polls are taken? We can have the Master skillfully plowing through our heart, we can fortify our windows, and the enemy is still "steadily" climbing into our house through the box in our living room! Do you realize this!? The article asked the question, "Has American television gone too far?" *YES! YES!* A resounding– YES! Certain film, music, and media are *extremely dangerous* to your house! The thief still lurks and waits for his entry through yours and your children's windows. He's desperate to kill your house and this is one of his most powerful tools of destruction!

The educated and the spirit-filled Christian may be "concerned," but WE SHOULD BE AT AN ALL OUT BATTLE STANCE against the types of media that capitalize on something that steals, kills, and destroys our houses! Mom and Dad, don't bring your child or your marriage to a pastor or counselor to be "fixed" if you're going to allow the thief to have this entry into your lives. We can't help you. For he works day and night tirelessly to destroy you, and you're letting him, one image at a time.

I'm radical about TV, video, computer, and music allowed into my house. Some people that I've loved dearly have made the statement, "Well, Angie, they're just going to see it somewhere else", or "they're going to see it sooner or later".

Have you told your children to look away? Have you explained to them about the broken gift? Have you told them about the thief who uses the mind's eye to draw us into destructive behavior? Behavior that destroys our right relationship with God and with each other? Have you said this to your children? Does someone need to convince you? Does your house understand fully that what enters the eye is engraved on the heart?

Because if you don't tell them, who *will*!? Someone also said to me once, "It just doesn't affect me that way." How selfish! First of all, I promise you it does! Because lust is part of the base nature of every human being! If by some chance you still believe the images and programming won't affect you, you should be concerned that someone with a broken gift is sitting in your living room! What's playing on your screen may be sending that someone spinning back into horrible battles with a thief who entered their house long ago!

If you have cable TV and unprotected Internet access, you or your family may not view the "junk", but even the "junk commercials" can damage a visitor's progress toward the building of their new house. And when God *saves* us, He *calls* us to watch over the spiritual well-being of our brothers and sisters in this world!

A new house the Master Artificer has worked carefully to design should never be threatened or undermined by things the beloved might be exposed to in our houses. And a neighbor's child's eyes should never behold things in our houses that our neighbor has been frantically trying to keep away! If this thief ever twists or breaks you or your child's gift, you'll know frantic protectiveness personally!

Oh how tired I am of these statements! And I'm tired of those who would say people with my point of view are just people threatened by the sexuality of others, or that we are just suppressed! Or church lady prim! – I am none of those! I am one who misses my family members who were supposed to be a healthy part of my life! And I grieve for the misery I've seen them living in! The house of the broken gift hurts! Horribly! The thief intended the murder to be painful!

In the September 2002 issue of <u>Time</u> magazine, there is an article about the increase of suicide attempts, especially in college students. In the thirty years from 1950 to 1980, the annual suicide rate among 19-24 year old women has almost doubled, from 3.9 deaths per 100,000 to 7.0 per 100,000, while the rate among young men has tripled from 10 per 100,000 to 32 per 100,000. The article states, "not all attempts are successful, but a person who's tried killing themselves once is at a greater risk of trying again." We ask why, and one of the answers is right there – engraved on their hearts! They don't have intimate soul to soul relationships – whole, healthy, and pure – with anyone! They only know the distorted and twisted misuse of the gift of sexuality. The resulting damage to the soul leaves them empty and in pain. And this is a pain for some, once so broken, which only death or the Master can relieve.

Last night, as I looked through my windows into my husband's windows, I saw him there. He looked through his windows into my windows and saw me there, seeing him. He said, "If we could pull our hearts out of our chests and lay them right here side by side between us, they'd have their arms and legs all wrapped up around each other!" He also calls the physical changes in me brought about by the birth of our children God's initials that are placed there to remind him of when He gave him his children! My husband and I often don't get past the other's windows. Physical appearances pale in comparison to the beauty of a soul. And this intimate soul to soul relationship satisfies the inner longing inside us. The Master seals that soul to soul relationship with completeness. God said it's not good for man to be alone – and the thief is well aware that the distortion of the gift leaves a man just that – alone.

I praise and thank my Lord for the truth and wholeness in my relationship with my husband today. I thank Him for the forgiveness and healing He so freely bestowed when the effects of the broken gift had destroyed my relationship with Him.

I give God all glory for the plowing of the junk from the table of my heart, and the Master design of my new house with extra large, beautiful, new windows. May nothing ever enter there again that can harm me or my loved ones. Bless His Name!

We love you, Jesus!

Amen.

Part 2 – Chapter 7

APPRAISAL NOT REQUIRED!

What would Eve have done with a credit card? Think about it!! Her eye was definitely on the best of the best! What she saw on that tree was pleasant to the eyes! And if one possessed <u>that</u> fruit – it would make one wise! Yes, Eve was a classic example of defining self-worth in possessing what the eyes behold!

I know many books have been written about the dangers of credit cards and increasing amounts of debt in a home, but I also see family after family continuing to struggle and miss the joy of a content and happy existence! Men and women falling prey to the same subtle message that initiated the very fall of man!

In the day you possess the fruit that is pleasant to the eyes you shall be as gods!

Genesis 3:5

You possess it = You're somebody!

And Adam and Eve, who walked in the garden with God, who were physically closer to God than any other people have ever been on this earth, still felt the need to possess more in order to be more! How much more so will the children who grew up in the House of the Pretty Purple Dress? The poor who knew only a bare and lonely existence with no brightness and no comfort! Give these adult parent-children credit and you've given them a means to be! The right clothes, the right shoes, the right restaurants, the right house, the right car -- we must possess them!

> *And the eyes of them both were opened and they knew that they were naked; and they sewed fig leaves together, and made themselves aprons.*
>
> *Genesis 3:9*

Once we possess it, it's never what we sought! So we get another boat, and a new couch, and a trip to the destination our neighbor took this summer is a must! And eventually we're sewing the fig leaves to cover what we've done -- to keep everyone from seeing what a desire to "*possess*" in order to "be" has actually become! A huge statement is in verse 17:

> *In sorrow shalt thou eat of it all the days of thy life – thorns also and thistles shall it bring forth to thee.*
>
> *Genesis 3:17*

Is this you, dear friend? It's sure been me at times in my life! The thorns and thistles have been long and sharp. Deep sorrow has accompanied the defeats of chasing personal worth, brightness of life and comfort in material things one could possess.

In your new house, precious friend, an appraisal of worth is not required. You see, in verse 21, God made coats of skins to clothe Adam and Eve. Only God knows our fig leaves will never cover the messes we've made just as He knew the fruit would never make a human become God. The people hiding in the mess behind the fig leaves are worth so much more than they understand! It took a sacrifice of life to make the coats of skin to cover Adam and Eve's prideful attempts to be more! God also made a sacrifice of life that covers all need to be somebody! And what He did for us, in His death, burial, and resurrection, was place a price on us far above what this world will ever comprehend. You see, God said we were worth His life first. He said it before we were born. We don't have to own or do or be anything. We just walk alongside Him in the garden

He's provided us, or enabled us to obtain thru honest labor, within our means, for our pleasure, but never to define us!

In the adult child/parent's need and search for significance, we can find so many bright and beautiful counterfeit appraisals! But we need only to look at the cross. No other words need to be said. It took the cross to buy us – and the cross was not too much for God to pay.

Who Are You?

Our only possession must needs be Jesus
No other thing defines
Who we are and what we're worth
Until the end of time.
Purple dresses with satin sleeves
Bring smiles when the world looks on.
But a cross on a hill brings Heaven's chorus
Crying out – "You are God's own!"
God's own child, with all of the claims as
An heir to all that He has!
You're rich in Christ!
You're worth His life!
A cross or a dress –

Who are you?

Part 3 – Chapter 1

THE ULTIMATE ARCHITECT

And God <u>said</u>, "Let there be light.":
<u>And there was light.</u>
Genesis 1:3

And God <u>said</u>, "Let there be a firmament in the midst of the waters, and let it divide the waters from the waters":
<u>and it was so.</u>
Genesis 1: 6 & 7

And God <u>said</u>, "Let the waters under the heaven be gathered together unto one place, and let the dry land appear":
<u>and it was so.</u>
Genesis 1:9

And God <u>said</u>, "Let the earth bring forth grass, the herb yielding seed, and the fruit tree yielding fruit after his kind whose seed is in itself, upon the earth":
<u>and it was so.</u>
Genesis 1:11

And God <u>said</u>, "Let there be lights in the firmament of the heaven to divide the day from the night; and let them be for signs and for seasons, and for days and years, and let them be for lights in the firmament of the heaven to give light upon the earth":
<u>and it was so.</u>
Genesis 1:14

And God <u>said</u>, "Let the waters bring forth abundantly the moving creature that hath life, and fowl that may fly above the earth; let the earth bring forth the living creature after his kind, cattle and creeping thing, and beast of the earth after his kind":

<u>and it was so.</u>
Genesis 1: 20 & 24

And God <u>said</u>, "Let us make man in our image after our likeness: And the Lord God formed man of the dust of the ground, and breathed into his nostrils the breath of life: <u>and man became a living soul.</u>
Genesis 1: 26, 2:7

When God speaks–all of creation listens and will not be still! The very sound of Him animates molecules and particles. They swirl and fly into patterns of beautiful design! Bringing into existence that which had no existence before He uttered its name! The following is a passage from <u>Signs of Design</u> by Carl Williand.

> "It is often overlooked that the properties of a cell which make it alive cannot be explained by just referring to the chemical properties of its building blocks."

In the same manner as this, the properties of my house which make it alive cannot be explained by just referring to the properties of its building blocks! My beautiful family is caused by intelligent design!

God awakened the building blocks of my house! It recognized it had a design to follow and was programmed to life! And things began to move and change and form and fly and exist where nothing existed before!

> *For thou, O Lord of Hosts,*
> *God of Israel, Hast revealed to thy servant saying,*
> *"I will <u>Banah</u>." And now, O Lord God,*
> *Thou art <u>that</u> God, And thy <u>words</u> be true –*
> *And thou hast <u>promised</u> this goodness*

> *Unto Thy servant: Therefore now let it please Thee to*
> *Bless the house of Thy servant, That it may continue ever before Thee–*
> *For Thou, O Lord God, Hast "SPOKEN" it.*

2 Samuel 7: 27 & 28

When the "Ultimate Architect" spoke the world into existence, things changed. Stillness, dark, and void could not ignore His command. Movement, light, and substance come forth! In these scriptures, God has spoken again. This time, it's not merely speaking – but the speaking of a promise: "I will Banah" (I WILL BUILD THEE A HOUSE!).

Banah is the word used here in the original Hebrew text. I almost fell over when I began to understand what God was showing me here! He is such an awesome Father! As I read and studied this new word, I found that God first used Banah in Genesis – when He formed Eve from Adam's rib! He was creating the first family! The first home!

This is the Banah promise! As I began to write this book, I prayed earnestly and carefully for God to show me how He brought me from my old house to my new one. Oh, the sweet precious presence I felt as He led me to the treasure of this promise! The Banah promise was already spoken when as a little girl my heart began to cry out to God for a home!

Dear friend, my house would have never had the life and strength and vitality, the awesome abundance of joy that it now has, had I not asked the Ultimate Architect to impose His intelligence

His word

    His knowledge

        His life!

            Upon it!

In a moment of time my house was awakened, and it realized it had a design to follow – it was programmed to live!! And then – only then – did things begin to move and change and exist where before there was nothing! There is something that I did – not knowing what I did – but now I'm finding it was a key factor in my life and receiving my Banah promise:

> Therefore hath thy servant found in his heart to pray this prayer unto thee –SINCE THOU HAS SPOKEN –concerning your servant's house – establish it forever and DO AS THOU HAS SAID for thou, O Lord God, HAST SPOKEN IT! Like David, we must <u>pray</u> for the <u>performance</u> of God's promise!
> <u>You</u> turn the <u>promise</u> into a <u>prayer</u> –
> <u>God</u> turns the <u>promise</u> into <u>performance</u>!
> With God, <u>saying</u> and <u>doing</u> are <u>not two different</u> things!

Banah includes: adding to existing material to fashion a new object, rebuilding something that is destroyed, and establishing,"fortifying" the house He builds us! This beautiful word – Banah – is what happened in my life. Until I set out to write this book and tell you, I didn't even know how to say it myself! God has performed the Banah promise that was spoken in the Word! I lived in the old neighborhood – house to house – year after year. I began to ask God for something that I had no idea was so clearly and specifically promised; and He has moved me into a brand new house in a brilliantly alive new neighborhood! Every change in my character, every ounce of strength, every step towards true normal, every day, every person of faith in my path-- all of it was the performance of His Banah promise! I love Him so much for this! He just never stops! Each and every time I lay my house before Him again, He takes us to yet a deeper and more warm love than we knew even the day before! Oh, how real his touch is! –and how He longs to touch every life He's created!

And it gets even better! The root words of Banah are Ben and Bat – son and daughter! When God promises, "I will Banah," He wasn't talking about my house alone! He was speaking a promise about the establishment of my children! And my children's children! Thank you, Father! Only you love them more than I do!

My heart's fervent prayer is that my children and grandchildren will walk before God! Like Hannah, in scripture, who "raised her son to stand before the Lord and serve in His temple," I hope I never miss a heartbeat of opportunity to teach them of His love! For if the Lord of Hosts, God of Israel, that God who spoke creation into existence establishes them, Oh, how firm a foundation! And what happiness in store!

Throughout this book I have spoken to you of warmth and love, security and peace, presence and power, and healing and value the Ultimate Architect offers to your house – free and clear.

A promise is graciously given – not bought.

I am mentally looking you square in the eye, my friend, young or old – gazing from the windows of my new house – declaring the realness of God and the permanent effects of His touch on my life and home. There is no other way from the sad, barren houses of my youth except He performed the Banah promise in my life! My new house is full of laughter; it is <u>good</u> to live here! Therefore, I know that I have received His ultimate blessing, here on earth, here in my house!

Everything we've talked about from start to finish, He has also promised to you! My writing began with one ultimate goal– that you will pray for the Banah promise to be performed in your life.

It was <u>spoken</u>

It will <u>be so!</u>

When you speak your faith in the performance of Banah in prayer, your whole world will begin to divide! and reshape! and bring forth new life! That, I know, may be hard for you to imagine – but He will delight in performing for you the deep and intricate desires of your heart – giving you above and beyond all that you can ask, think, or imagine.

The Banah promise – spoken by the Ultimate Promise Keeper –

performed by the Ultimate Architect of the ages – What else is needed to build one's house?

Nothing, my friend…

Now, pray for the Banah promise to be performed in your life!

God can create something out of nothing. He can restore and add to existing structures, or He can completely start anew. It doesn't matter, the promise is spoken. It will be so. His ways are higher than our ways, and the others in your house may refuse. Just trust Him. His performances are worth the wait. Place all expectations in Him, and He will delight in you!

Part 3 – Chapter 2

MAINTENANCE AND UPKEEP

In the final chapters of Banah, God led me to offer you some guidelines to help you as you're moving into your new neighborhood. I have watched people through the years – both individuals and families – who receive new understanding with a bang spiritually, and then fizzle out. I am so concerned about our faith. We seem to be effective in sharing the gospel, but not as effective in leading others into spiritual maturity needed to cope with day to day life. I recently spoke with a teacher who teaches in a local Christian school, a Bible class to students in grades 10-12. At the beginning of a recent school year, only one young adult in all the classes could identify Abraham! This blows my mind! If you asked the parents of these kids, I know each of them would tell you they have a 'Christian' home!

Please hear this! When God turns His promise into performance in your house – there is a spiritual principal you must grasp at once -- Maintenance and Upkeep!!! Many words define maintenance: "to rule", "to guide the house", "to stand before", "to lead", "to attend its needs with care and diligence". Biblically speaking, the beginning of a rule and the ability to maintain it begins at conversion. So, my friend, the ability and obligation to stand before your household and lead it came to you when you sealed your relationship with Love!

When you invited Him into your life, when you opened the door to your house and He entered in,
when He "imposed His divine knowledge on your properties," when the oil tempered the clay, the ability to attend to the needs of your house and lead it was given to you!

To maintain your house you must lead with diligence! You must diligently apply yourself to understanding the Bible! If you can't understand the Bible, find a mentor! Keep looking until you can find someone to speak your heart to! Don't be afraid to ask questions!

Precept upon precept, attend to the needs of your house! Learn and teach! To lead also means to "bear" or "carry". Will you carry each need to the ultimate source for it to be met?

I've recently watched the movie "John Q". At the beginning, when the son falls on the ballfield and Denzel Washington is carrying him – running for help – my tears fall, my heart aches.

I know how many thousands of families are facing those same job cutbacks!
Those unpaid bills! Those things that build and build! A child is sick! No insurance! People <u>trying</u> to lead! Trying to carry their house to a place of hope and healing!

I <u>promise</u> you that at this point there are no words to write! But, there is a <u>God in heaven!</u> And this is where the rubber meets the road in your faith! John Q. Archibald led his house! Oh that we would lead ours so radically to the throne!

And the upkeep! Keepers are those who guard and protect. The time that my house is allowed in this world is my watch! I must search out and expose any weaknesses. I must fortify it and strengthen it. I will not allow myself to become slack on my watch!

I have a house. I also have an enemy – a thief – who will destroy my house in a heartbeat for the sheer evil joy of seeing me and my loved ones suffer! I dare not become lazy!

But with all vigilance – and all bravery – and all human attempts at fortification, I realize that all of my attempts are futile unless I pray like David did in Psalms 141:3…

"Set a watch, O Lord…"

We must ask God to set a watch and allow His grace to keep our house! We will need <u>extreme</u> amounts of <u>grace</u> for this precious watch! And therefore we must understand how to get extreme amounts of grace!

God giveth grace to the humble-Humble yourselves therefore…

I Peter 5:5 & 6

So how do we get more grace? We get on our knees! And live by the fact that we no longer have a will of our own! Every moment in life is humbly submitted to the sovereign will of God! If God says do it– do it! It's that simple! This is humbling ourselves, bowing ourselves and our will before Him. And as a result, the grace will flow freely for the upkeep, for the <u>watch,</u> of everything we hold dear! Oh, how desperately we need grace!

> And once again – Praise Him for His Plan!
> Praise Him for His Provision!
> Praise Him for His love!
> And praise Him for life!

With maintenance and upkeep – and the grace it affords – you'll never fizzle! But every day of your spiritual life will be filled with bang after bang after bang! Your house will stand even though storms rage against it and weaknesses within threaten to fold it! My husband and I stand amazed every day, amazed at how much stronger our house is each day than even the day before! We *know* it's nothing of our own strength…it is the effect of God's presence, plain and simple! But we also realize His presence brings with it a *call* on our lives, a call to *maintain* and *keep* what He's established! This call is on the life of *every* believer. So, my friend, what will be your answer to the call?

Will you humbly lead and keep your watch through grace? May we never grow slack! May we never forget the houses we came from! Being brought from there is all I need to pledge my whole heart and life on my knees in efforts to maintain and upkeep all that God has given. Luke 12:48 says to whom much is given, much is required. I also say to whom much is given, much overflows back to whence it came! This is not a requirement; it's an aftereffect! No, I cannot rest quietly soaking up the goodness of life and not go back after others! To just sit on it would be so wrong! I may spend my whole life trying to carry back to God human tokens of gratitude for His love. Each one of you I can connect to Him is my way of saying, "I love you" to

Him and to you. I know the delight of His heart is a relationship with <u>you!</u> And a relationship with Him will delight your heart in return! So I am passionately trying to tell you of His great love and will attempt to lovingly carry you before the throne each day! Hoping always that you will receive the grace to stay there! It comes thru maintenance and upkeep alone, my friend, maintenance and upkeep! And a job requirement for this labor of love is the ability to get down on our knees. Arthritic pride is the excuse in many lives for shabby maintenance and upkeep, but the remedy for stiff knees is to bend them more often – and the more often you bend – the freer the movement and the less painful it becomes! It's your choice, use it or lose it! Losing grace. Now that's a scary thought! Come to think of it, I don't believe you really have a choice at all!

Part 3 – Chapter 3

THE HOUSE WITH THE STEEPLE

My church has loved me through everything that has touched my life. As a small child, they sang to me. They were warm and safe for the short times I could be with them. I rode in the white Ford pick-up with my great-grandfather, VERY SLOWLY (he didn't like fast) one mile up the highway to the red brick house with a tall white steeple on top. It's the one house I can remember with a smile.

And later, when my life was so much less than spotless, my church smiled at me and spoke to me of love. They called and they reached. If ever I was bound and determined to fall, they evermore were bound and determined to break that fall!

When I married, though money was scarce, I lacked nothing. My church gave everything required to set up housekeeping, everything from dishes to sheets to towels to pillowcases…everything.

When my children were born, they gave *everything* once again – car seat, swing, bassinet, toys, clothes, and this time, home-made crocheted blankets and booties!

When my grandparents went home to be with God, they brought casseroles and hams, rolls and pies and cakes, and they also brought wisdom to understand eternity and where my granddaddy <u>really</u> was. They sang to me again, and the same warmth and safety flowed in the midst of grief.

And when my mother's husband was taken in an accident, swiftly and suddenly, deep in the night, they came – all of them – 3 AM – standing in my kitchen. The women led my mother by hand through the days and weeks that followed. The men mowed her yard, fed her cows, and took care of things left undone.

I've heard people say they can know God and worship God from their living room or their fishing boat, so there is no need for church. But there is so much more to the house with the steeple! There is such beauty in being a part of this house God uses to carry His song of life to others! He meets needs through the house with the steeple!

He loves through the house with the steeple!

My church has the same problems as Any Church, USA, but I'm convinced the problems are shallow and insignificant in comparison to the way that they love!

You must lead your new house regularly to the house with the steeple! There you will find others in need and you'll be found in yours!

I attended a Chonda Pierce concert last year - I just love her! – and I've got to tell you something I saw. I was sitting in the nosebleed section, the place where when you look out at the light fixtures that you are eye level with you feel faint! When the concert was over, those lights came on and in the row in front of me sat seven senior, very senior, citizens! I thought, "How on earth did they get up here?" And then, "How on earth will they get down?" Just as I was about to call 911 - because I knew they were about to need it! – I saw seven Senior Saints become the house with the steeple before my eyes! They took three steps at a time – consecutively downward. Six lined up on either side of the steps – three by three. The one remaining at the top would go down the middle holding onto the others as they held on to her. When she got to the end, she took a place and another one from the top proceeded down in the same fashion. They repeated this – slowly but surely – all the way down. I promise you, if one fell down, they all were going! They held on with such care! They leaned in! And they coached one another with words of encouragement all the way down! That's us, folks! The house with the steeple. That's how we get through life. We hold on! We lean in! We coach one another! And if one falls – we all fall!

People with darkness in their lives and in their hearts have marred the name of our precious churches. For many Americans the word church brings to mind thoughts and memories too horrible to mention. This means we must seek ways to love more, reach farther, and simply do what we do! Good will always overcome evil, because dark cannot, has not, and will NEVER consume the light!

In a way, the actions of a few have caused our house with the steeple to stumble, teetering on the edge of a seemingly unavoidable fall. We must hold on – lean in – and coach the church on with positive words of encouragement! As long as it takes -- no matter the cost!

The darkness of a few cannot be allowed to continue tearing down our precious house with the steeple! She loves too much! She gives too much! She sings too beautifully with flowing warmth and love!

You lead your *new* house to her, dear friend, and I'll lead mine there, too! We'll grab hold of her, lean in, and love like never before in all of history! – Since the first one was built so long ago! Our goal will be to overtake the darkness with the light of the truth! And we won't rest – we won't stop – until the name of our precious house with the steeple is safely restored!

Unmarred!

Beautiful!

And strong!

She's done it for us – Let's do it for her!

Part 3 – Chapter 4

UNRIVALED SOUTHERN HOSPITALITY

Down here, where I come from, you must expect you're gonna get a visit or two every day! We stop by to drink coffee in the morning, we borrow lawn mowers and sugar in the afternoon, and in the evening we cook out or just git together and talk on the porch! I figure somewhere or other in the course of this book you've probably figured out I'm from the South! But I promise you, they put the ones who talk really slow on the news on purpose! You know how the TV adds ten pounds to your weight? Well it REALLY slows your speech down, too! So there! I'm finally telling the truth about our accent!

All jokes aside, I think you'll find something very similar to our unrivaled southern hospitality in your new neighborhood. You'll see that the incredible joy of these "Banah" houses flows out into the community around them. It is joy that can't be contained! As I wrote in the beginning chapter, I couldn't stay in my house another day and not invite you to come inside! Maybe that's Southern -- I've been told by colleagues in various business travels that I fit their mental picture of a Southern Belle. Somehow I can't picture me in a hoop skirt! But the drawl and the invitations for others to come into my house -- I've got that part down pat!

My favorite guests are those that I am pretty sure live in the old houses. I can usually spot them at once – remember the bull in the china shop clumsy feeling? That's so evident on their faces! At once I begin to pull out the food, the cokes, the laughter, anything my pea-brain can grasp to make them feel at ease and at home in this house! You see, I've got to become their friend. I must let them feel the incredible joy in this new neighborhood – for they have no other way of knowing this life! We must be gracious. We must cover their clumsiness and, if something in our house is bumped into – knocked over – or stepped on – (this can be our feelings, my friend!) we must overlook it! Cover it! Let them know it's okay to bump and stumble around in this house! Until they feel safe and comfortable! Until they can begin to trust that the joy can be for them too! This was done for me and I'll never forget it!

This is more than being Southern. This is the seed of compassion planted in us and growing in us to the point of overflow! This was yet another call placed on our house when we did business with the Ultimate Architect! It's vital! *"Go ye therefore and tell somebody else!"* You cannot move into your new house in your new neighborhood and become a hermit! You must invite those from the old neighborhoods, bring them inside to experience the Banah promise. You must never take personal credit for the beauty and grandeur of your home – but carefully and gently lead them to the One who built it!

And there should be no hospitality anywhere that rivals the hospitality found in your house with the steeple! I truly believe this house should be the most well-kept, grandiose, and beautiful house in your community! But the muddiest feet and the dirtiest hands should be welcomed with smiles and warmth! Remember, there's a powerful sacrifice in this house that will blast away any stains once applied! How could we ever feel that the original condition of our own hands and feet was any more acceptable or welcome? No! Never! We welcome with a gracious smile all those who would awkwardly or boldly step inside! What occurs after that is between the Architect and the occupant! We don't appraise the guest. An appraisal was not required of us! Our responsibility is to invite, greet, share, and introduce.

But what if these people are our parents, grandparents, aunts, or uncles from all those years ago? Birthdays, Christmas, and Thanksgiving can now be just as uncomfortable, sad, and difficult as in the old neighborhood. I've got to address this for you.

Hang on, it's another one of those strange dreams. I don't know why dreams have such a profound effect on me – I'm so sheep-like! I think it could be some of the best really still time God has to talk to me. I dreamed I was inside my house alone. My husband was at work and my children were at school. A man came into my yard and walked right up to my front door. I looked through my window and saw him advance across the yard. I managed to bolt the door quickly and grab the phone, quietly rushing to hide in the back of my house. I dialed my mother's number. She answered. In a voice filled with panic, I told her of the man at the door. I begged her – please come! Come quickly! She said, "I'm not coming out there right now – I don't have time! It's probably just a salesman." I was frozen with fear, begging her, "please come, please". Then I heard the man at the back door. Looking out, I saw he had tools, diligently working to loosen the lock and reverse the bolt! So I began to beg my mother, "Please call my husband. Please tell him! Tell him to come – come quickly!" I was crying and begging, still holding the phone, when the door opened wide and the thief stepped in. I choked out, "Why are you here?" He smiled and quietly said, "I've come to kill you."

Now why do you suppose in this dream I called my mother? Why not 911? Because, dear friend, God was revealing to me a wonderful truth about Banah – His establishment of my house.

Lord, help me share this carefully! I believe this is what we all feel about those people who missed their divine appointment to love us, teach us, and protect us in the old neighborhood. Way down deep inside, we're still holding that phone and our heart cries, Why? Why didn't you come? The thief came in and took our relationship! He killed our mother-daughter bond! Our father-daughter relationship will never be! Our father-son bond stolen! Our mother-son relationship murdered! And if we allow ourselves to think too long – we withdraw and hide from these people for the rest of our lives. If they left us bare before the thief all those years ago, then coming close to them now brings us incredibly close to the pain of the thief's slow murder again and again. I asked God why I called my mother in this dream and not my father? It's because God has gloriously changed her life and brought her into a loving relationship with me now, but the thief would still desire to steal it. It's still in danger. He's at our door – anxious to kill! God builds the house. Satan destroys it. In your new house, one of your weakest fortifications will be the present-day relationships with the people from the old houses.

There is no guilt like a mother's guilt. Every single day, mothers turn to the Light and sin is dealt with. Forgiveness and mercy are understood and received through layer after layer of those generational mistakes and sins. The healing and restoring penetrate and renew her life –

until the layer is reached where a woman knows she has wronged her child.

I was afraid and nauseated the day I gave Banah to my mother for the very first time. I knew God was telling me to write about these things, but I was afraid of hurting her. I know God can't use this book to help others if it hurts my mother.

After reading it, my mom told me she felt nauseated – and as we talked, she began to cry.

She said, "I'm the one who did this to you. I'm the one who left you alone!"

I said, "Mother, I have new windows. I see the generational layers you both were lost in. I see what God is doing right now."

She said, "I don't remember any of it. That period of my life is erased from my memory."

I asked my mother if there was any part of this book she would have me leave off. I wanted to leave nothing in it that would make her uncomfortable.

She immediately responded, "No!" I said, "Are you sure?"

Again, an emphatic, "No, nothing." Here was a beautiful performance of Banah – happening even as Banah was being written.

She felt me see her love of the Light.

Heaven's love spilled out of her, and fused with love spilling out of me – even now continuing to heal and restore. I began to understand how mothers and daughters bond in adulthood, in spite of the past.

God says condemnation is this only:

To love the dark and hate the light.

John 3: 19-20

My mother hates the dark of those old houses. My mother loves the Light that came into the world. Therefore, the thief has to take his tool of condemnation, and leave the door of our new house – for his condemnation has been exposed by her love of the Light!

My mother's blank space, or lack of memories is not uncommon. The testimony of many people from the old neighborhood is the same. They became so good at pretending things didn't happen, and putting forth that false normal façade, their minds so blocked it all that they began to believe it <u>didn't</u> happen. It's a coping mechanism formed in order to survive, just like all the others. And we had to survive. But something in the blank space still makes my mother cry. And I don't want what happened then to have the power to make my mother cry now! Could it be that locked away in the pretend world of 'didn't happen' means it is left to the thief to use against us? To steal, kill, and destroy what we have now? I believe so.

God takes a past that makes us cry and turns it into testimony. No more tears – but words about the Promise of His healing and restoration!

No. I do not think it's necessary that details be remembered or discussed. I do think it is very necessary to say to God in prayer, "Lord, you know what is there in my mind and heart – and I want you to have control of it. It's yours, Lord. Don't let it harm me or be used against me."

To revisit and reveal some of the houses of this book is not easy! It's very painful. But there was no hesitancy when I asked my mother to revisit the pain to help me go after others. There was no hesitancy at all. Only heaven's Love spilling out of her and fusing with the Love spilling out of me.

The layer of self-condemnation she carried for so many years was dissolving between us – for she felt me see her love of the Light. In this, there is no condemnation.

Mothers, you love Jesus with all your heart. That's all you need to do! You do not have to keep asking your child to forgive you over and over again! Just love Jesus and let them see you doing that!

Adult child/parents, you let your mothers feel you seeing them love Jesus! You tell them you see them love Jesus! The same fusing of God's love I've told you about throughout flows from you both and bonds you! It's God again. Nothing more. Nothing less. Loving Him corrects all – heals all – restores all. No more crying.

God has answered the "Why my mom didn't rescue me then?". Layers – generational layers of the 'stuff'. The Sacrifice has defeated the "why." Felt it, faced it, defeated it, restoring and healing the damage. The Sacrifice dissolves the lump – clears the chest to love freely through the new windows. The new windows we peer at these people through are very different. We no longer see them just as our parents, grandparents, aunts, and uncles. We see them as the those in need of a new house. That's what they are, dear friend, homeless, as far as warmth and love is concerned. Just as we were before the Ultimate Architect. Birthdays and Christmas we prepare for them, the same way we would any homeless person on the street. We turn the lamp God has placed inside us on. We prepare the banquet. And we open the door.

Now, they may not come. And often, if they come it will be on their terms, and they may bring the old baggage with them. But if you've been in the Word – you'll be a mirror reflection of God's image. His presence will be there in the countenance of your face, which means they'll begin to be in His presence!

Many times you won't have to say a word to them! His presence goes before you, and does all the talking that's needed! The lamplight shines and its glow falls softly over all who are present. When their words fall carelessly or cause discomfort, hear with spiritual ears! Hear the layers – remember the power of the sacrifice you're trying to bring into their life! These things are only possible through the transforming power of the Holy Spirit in you. Your intimate time with Him is the <u>only</u> thing that will ever make your face different. You and Him. Alone. Nothing more. Nothing less.

The Bible says, "Honor your father and mother." There is no grading scale. There are no conditions. God just says do it. It is our responsibility to be right with God. It has nothing whatsoever to do with their performance in our lives. You see, it places us in a very powerful position for God to draw them to Himself through us. Now,

I believe there are definite boundaries put in place here by other parts of God's Word. Lying, stealing, misuse and distortion of the gift of intimacy – none of these are to be compromised in order to honor our father and mother. To use every opportunity afforded to bring them to the new neighborhood, this is honor. To be respectful when speaking to them, this is honor. To be sure they have food, clothes, and shelter as they age, this is honor. To pay a bail bondsman to get them out of jail for another DUI, drug-related charge, or assault, this is not honor. This is codependency. Honor is to visit the jail – love them through the windows – see that they have food – and speak to them of a promise. But do not pay their way out of jail into the next mistake. This is not honor, and it is not going to lead them anywhere. It becomes their stepping stone to the next blow from the thief in the murder of their house. Avoid being that stepping stone at all costs. It is not honor. It destroys them. God says consequences – adversity – will teach them. Let it. It can mean life or death!

And what about yesterday's parent-children who now have God's glorious presence and healing in their lives, but are missing the overflowing joy because of the fat, heavy guilt sitting squarely on their brain and on their chest? There is no condemnation in Christ Jesus. None. Notta. Gone. Jesus did not come to condemn the world, but to save it. The sacrifice dissolves it. God's presence replaces the guilt with thanksgiving and gratefulness because <u>God</u> saves! God frees! There's no freedom to praise when your focus is guilt! Send the guilt back to hell where it came from and begin thanking God for your new house! Then those you feel guilty about letting down will see your new house is real! Now get on with it! Put off the guilt and put on the praise! This new house has <u>never</u> been about what we did or didn't do, but what He's done and continues to do! Get it? Focus <u>off</u> you and <u>on</u> Him! <u>He</u> is what changes all lives!

The thief's tools include condemnation and guilt, fear of old pain, and unforgiveness. He uses them to break the fortification of our new house and enter neighborhoods just like the old once again. Yes, he will skulk and sneak and work his way into the new. We <u>must</u> take those tools out of his possession and place them at the cross – under the Sacrifice. God's healing prevents the old hurt from ever hurting again, and His power enables us to live the 70 X 7 rule in our hearts – not just with our mouths. Remember the disciples asked how many times do we forgive? And Jesus, plainly answers 70 X 7? This symbolizes a complete and infinite number, meaning it is beyond us – beyond our comprehension – therefore not something we can 'do'. God does it – in us and through us – the same way He does everything else.

My precious neighbor, I've written so many words to say something so incredibly and beautifully simple. Jesus.

That one solitary life impacted our world like a blazing comet in the night! God on earth releasing the power to transform entire personalities! Entire families! Entire cities! Entire nations! And the world! The power He blazed into this world through that sacrifice will always and forevermore stand between my new house and the thief. My parents couldn't – Jesus could. And He is. And He always will.

This is the hope. It is the hope for me, my children, my parents, and my grandparents. It is the hope for you, your children, your parents, and your grandparents. He stands ready to perform the Banah promise in all lives. All, whosoever. He is the hope of us all. He is gracious, and His hospitality is unrivaled. Neither, then, should ours be.

Christmas and birthdays – until now you may have dreaded these. But no more, once you fully grasp the hospitality of the God who has transformed you. Trust God and open your doors to those who truly are still 'homeless' in your life. Memorize the poem at the end of this chapter – and go live it!

Come to think of it, maybe that is a little bit of the South in me coming out in my story! But my Father is God of the North, South, East, and West! He performs the Banah promise all over this world! He invites all people of every nation to dwell in this new neighborhood. The Banah promise knows no barriers of race, creed, nationality, or language! His is truly unrivaled hospitality. Not only an invitation, but a plan, a provision, an establishment and a dwelling place to abide from now on for the rest of our days until the ultimate abiding is realized when we at last dwell in Him!

Hospitality

Butterbeans and cornbread,
fried pork chops, tomato soup,
biscuits and gravy.
Loaning your weedeater, your jumper cables,
your tractor, your lap top –

Whatever it takes to show them you're real,

That's what you do!

Turn a deaf ear to bad language,
Turn a blind eye to immodest dress,
Turn a closed mouth to the dirty laundry.

Instead,
Hear the old neighborhood in their voices –
Turn your eyes upon Jesus –
And speak to them of a promise!

Unrivaled Southern Hospitality!

Part 3 – Chapter 5

"WE DWELL IN HIM!"

The following is paraphrased from passages of scripture located in II Corinthians 5: 1-4 and Revelation 21 & 22.

> For we know that if our earthly house of this tabernacle were dissolved, we have a building of God, an house not made with hands, eternal in the heavens. For in this we groan, earnestly desiring to be clothed upon with our house which is from heaven. If so be that being clothed we shall not be found naked. For we that are in this tabernacle do groan, being burdened, not for, that we would be unclothed; but clothed upon, that mortality might be swallowed up of life.
>
> And John, the apostle, saw the holy city, the new Jerusalem, coming down from God out of heaven.
>
> And John heard a great voice out of heaven that said, "Look, see the <u>house</u> of God is with men, and He will <u>dwell</u> with them, and they will be His, and God Himself will <u>be with</u> them, and be their God.
>
> And God will wipe away all tears from their eyes – there will be no more death, or sorrow, or crying, or pain; <u>for the things of the old neighborhood are passed away</u>.
>
> The new dwelling will have light like a jasper stone, clear as crystal; and the wall of the neighborhood has <u>twelve foundations</u> – those <u>foundations</u> are trimmed with all manner of precious stones
>
> > The first – jasper
> > The second – sapphire

The third – chalcedony
The fourth – emerald
The fifth – sardonyx
The sixth – sardius
The seventh – chrysolite
The eighth – beryl
The ninth – topaz
The tenth – crysoprasus
The eleventh – jacinth
The twelfth – amethyst.

Every gate is a pearl – and <u>the streets of the neighborhood are pure gold.</u> And John saw <u>no house with a steeple,</u> for the Lord God Almighty and the Lamb are themselves the temple of the neighborhood! <u>This neighborhood has no need of the sun or the moon</u> – for the glory of the Lamb is the light! And in no way will anything enter it which will defile it! And we shall see His face!...

These sayings are <u>faithful</u> and <u>true</u> – the Lord God sent his angel to show John the way things will be!

I could have used the houses of my old neighborhood as an excuse for continuing to have a difficult life. Placing blame and gaining sympathy from others for the way our life is today has its advantages – it brings concern from others that we desperately need. Pastors, teachers, doctors, counselors, and friends will always listen to the story of where we've been and where we are. And they'll hold our hands, pray with us, teach us, give us prescriptions, and even help us with our bills – so leaning on the crutch of the old neighborhood becomes itself a house in that neighborhood! We may not be living the exact lives of our loved ones before us, but we are not free. We still dance as the thief plays the tune of the victim in our ear. This is where I find many adult 'child/parents' and 'parent-children' who talk to me today. You've made it out of the early houses, but you're still dancing as the tune of the victim plays in your head.

I hope you understand that Banah has not only been about building your house and your family, it's been about building you. I've been where you are, adult child/parent. I know about the basement, the attic, the closets. I know the hard stuff first-hand.

And I love you.

"Love your neighbor." Jesus Himself asked me to love you. He said this was the most important thing I could do after He loved me! So I began to tell those in my church what He did for me. After that, He gave me the opportunity to travel to many other audiences, even a local home for disadvantaged children. Then He blessed me with the privilege to volunteer at a wonderful Biblical counseling office, and yet I still felt inadequate – the need to tell more and more people about the Banah promise performed in my life continues to grow! Almost every tear-streaked face sitting across from me needs to hear and it's just impossible to get it all said in a few hour-long counseling sessions! As a result of God's leading me to share my story with more and more people, you are now holding Banah in your hands.

I'm praying that it's a divine appointment ordained by our Father that you are holding it. I'm praying you'll finish Banah and understand your dependence on and need for faith better than ever before in your life. I pray you'll allow Him to change you from victim to victorious.

And I want your joy to be increased again and again, resting in the knowledge that His Banah promise is not just for this world. He has also built for us a place to live for all eternity – after the clay and the earth are gone – we'll live where the walls are encrusted with jewels! And the roads are paved with gold! A place where the light of God's presence surrounds us and "keeps" us. We'll dwell in Him, for His light and His life will <u>give us life forever!</u> There will be no more crying, or sorrow, or pain. We'll see His face every day – with that countenance of passion fixed upon us! His eyes! We will see His eyes! Revealing His inward thoughts and feelings toward us! Can you imagine?

I've been told, "Well, it's good that it can be this way for you – but it's just not meant to be that way for some of us."

Here's another southern term for you --

"BULL"

My God, the god, who wrote the Book, said over and over and over again in that Book "all", "any", "whosoever" – I know very little about the hair-splitting of Calvin or Luther – but I know my Father, and a lot of the Book he wrote! That Book has taught me again and again-- it doesn't matter where you've been or where you are…it matters what you do with Jesus! The Sacrifice! Love that spilled and fused with the clay and blasts away everything that separates you from changing neighborhoods!

We will dwell in Him. In His presence. In His glory. At that moment of exiting this world will be the ultimate changing neighborhoods. He will be our light, our warmth, everything for our eternal life will be before Him – in that city – on golden highways – with no churches – for He is the *"temple of it"*.

Let me tell you what I did with Jesus -- I called out to him. I understood He is much more qualified to order my life than I am, and I wanted Him to order it. There came a point in my life when I understood exactly who Jesus was, that His sacrifice was for my blemished and unperfect clay, and I placed all of my faith and hope for this life and afterwards in Him—His sacrifice—His resurrection. I approached Him through the love behind the sacrifice, and the power released in the ressurection allowed me near Him. I wanted, and asked His presence to be a part of me – His spirit – Him – offered freely to me! Now my spirit is brilliantly alive in the warmth of Him! Ever changing, ever progressing toward His physical presence. You see, I didn't do a great or difficult thing, actually, I did nothing at all but receive a gift. Love did it all! Everything. Made it. Planned it. Wrapped it. Lived it. Gave it. Resurrected it. Offered it. *Freely*. For all eternity.

We simply understand who He is, and accept His precious offer to infuse us with Himself – cleansing and blasting – restoring and healing – die to ourselves to follow His presence and His teaching.

Call him boss. Worship Him with our mouths before others and join a house with a steeple so that we can learn of Him! The moment we place our faith in Him- place our lives in His hands – our dwelling place in heaven is yet another Banah promise! The most beautiful houses ever created will be there – for we shall be changed! We shall be like Him! We will stand before Him and not be melted like wax, for we shall be changed! No more clay – but glory! Have you done this in your life? His presence is before you in this moment. Ask Him now. Please don't let generational layers of life stand between you and love . Give Him the life He's given you. It's powerful. It's beautiful. And you are never alone again.

So we see creation began with God performing the Banah promise, and throughout time, he delights in continuing Banah in every life, and in the end – the ultimate Banah promise of all – Heaven.

A final house,
    A glorious house,
        Perfect and pure -
            Brilliant and alive.

All because long ago – God said it – and it is so.

Thank you for reading Banah. It's my first book and the content is precious to me. I think I've learned as much about these truths as anyone as I wrote them to you! I've had some of the sweetest and most precious moments of my Christian life in the quietness of my den with my Bible, my Savior, my pen, and my notepad. For your reading it, I humbly thank you. My closest prayer-warrior friends have been praying as I wrote and God has dealt genuinely with me about every line on every page. I believe with everything that I am in God's ability, willingness, and power to build our house. This sounds simple – too simple – but the way I moved out and learned to deal with those people and circumstances in my life was simply this: <u>time with Him.</u> There are no single or certain scriptures – no documentable facts – no lists – no medicines – no antidepressants. Nothing. Just results. And words can't define 'how'. I have asked you in every chapter to pray- talk to Him – pray – learn of Him – pray – understand Him – and that is the concrete, rock-solid, action you need in your life today. Nothing else in this world will ever make a real difference. Only what you can soak into yourself of Him! The One who speaks the promise! I want the life-changing understanding of the Banah promise to spread like wildfire – reclaiming homes and families, establishing them, and giving them a joy unspeakable.

There is one more thing I would ask of you. Share the Banah promise with someone in your neighborhood. You can reach those that I will never know! And every adult parent-child, every child/parent, needs to hear this message of hope – the promise of a house.

Again, thank you, and I love you. May the peace and free love of God be found in your house today!

POST NOTE

Banah was finished. The corrections were made, the typing was in progress, and my excitement was growing as I had begun to see God working in the lives of those who read the rough drafts. I knew God would always continue the performance of His promise in my life. But I had no idea how soon my need for it would grow to monstrous proportions. On 11/21/02, the thief played an ace. Life was stolen again in my family as the years of generational wrongs culminated in an event that I know the thief delighted in. The newspaper said, "The life of a 76-year-old man was taken by his son with a single gunshot wound to the chest." That son was my father. The 76-year-old man was my grandfather. The writers for the newspaper and the reporters for the local news couldn't see all that I could see. They missed the suffering affection, the abuse, the anger, the years upon years of generational layers of bitter and harsh.

God is so faithful. In the days following, I knew in my heart that I had to write for you how God worked in my life on that horrible day. I am amazed, still, at the reality of God's presence in my life on this earth.

The phone calls came quickly. Sobs and hysterical grief bursting through one call followed immediately by taut, high-pitched fear from another call. Understanding of the gravity of the situation settled down on my soul like the firm pulling pressure of a river current. Lost, disoriented, garbled – these words mildly describe my response. I knew nothing, but hitting my knees was my now-learned automatic reaction. There was no hesitation. No doubt. I knew where the rock was.

But this time, clinging to the rock, bowed down there underneath the feeling and circumstances, I had no voice! I couldn't speak to my Lord! I opened my mouth and nothing would come! These were moments frozen in my mind as those when true and utter dependence on the unseen comes full face before the believing heart.

My voice failed me that day, but a supernatural miracle occurred within my body. My right hand discovered a life of its own. Unlike my normal position for prayer, I raised it above my bowed head. Once it was there, my faltering voice began to catch the wind of His Spirit. At first, the words were whispered, broken, and fragile – then as my right hand slowly straightened into the air my voice became loud and strong! Oh, how I cried out for God to help us! I told Him of our desperate need, and asked Him to show me what to do. I acknowledged complete inability to get up off the floor unless He saw fit to raise me.

So get up off the floor is exactly what I did. I went straight to the scene where the ace was played. Speaking with law enforcement officials, holding broken loved ones, asking and answering questions, offering anything I had to try to help those who were left needing.

And then I went to the place where my father was being held – a building with rooms and bars. Bars over doors as well as the windows. These bars were to keep evil from getting out, rather than in. Bars to hold my father in. And once again the old need to explain to everyone how wrong they were was surfacing in my heart! I wanted to scream, "But you don't see the layers! You don't know how many word-bullets and fist-bullets were fired long before today!" Please know, I understand this ace. The word murder is ever before me!

God's gentle mercy surrounded us that day, and I was able to speak to my father. There was no anger or condemnation. There was a lot of fear. We spoke to him words of love and encouragement, and then had to leave him there, alone and separated from everything dear to him.

The day ended with fatigue. My husband fell asleep around midnight. By 1 AM, I had begun to grieve. I think this would be described as a soul in travail. I was hurting so deeply – groaning and crying – unable to stop the waves of sorrow from coming again and again. Trying to pray, the only word formed from the grief was "Help". That's all I could do. I repeated, over and over, Help! God, please Help! I stumbled out of bed and made my way to my Bible downstairs. Turning on the lamp, I repeated in my heart, over and over, Help – Please – Help!

I opened my Bible, and God led me straight to Isaiah 41:9 –
*Thou whom I have taken from the ends of
the earth.*

That's me. Remember crying from the ends of the earth in normal façade?
> *Fear not. I am with thee: be not dismayed,
> for I am thy God. I will strengthen thee; yea, I will
> help thee.*

> *For I the Lord thy God will hold thy right
> hand, saying unto thee, Fear not; I will
> help thee.*

> *Isaiah 41:13*

Wow!

God took me back to earlier the afternoon before when on my knees my self had gotten stuck in the mire, and my right hand went up with a life of its own. That was Him. Ever before me – in place before I called – saving His child unable to save herself. And when I didn't understand what He had done, He gently let the Word speak and explain the miracle taking place. It is the most direct and immediate answer I have ever received. My heart has to stop here and twirl for a minute in praise and worship of the One who loves me so! Thank you, Father.

There will be rooms with bars, and courtrooms, legal offices, and institutions in the future. All of these buildings could loom with menace and threats if I didn't know about the help and the right hand.

I will not enter these rooms armed with arguments and medications. Instead, I will be armed with His presence, my knowledge of the Lamb, and the sword of His Spirit which is my Bible itself. When the rooms are empty and my grief leaks in streams down my face, and chin, and neck, soaking the collar of my clothing, my comfort will come when I open my bible to Isaiah 41:13 and hold those words to my chest. Hugged across my heart, His word permeates deep inside to my innermost parts. His Spirit diffuses the pain, unclogs my chest and the leak is fixed again for a while. The clay is frail, and soon another leak may break through. But my Father's Spirit and His word will deal with the confusion, grief, anger, and sadness that attempt to clog my chest and prevent my normal function in life. Therefore, by His grace, I will live in a "true normal" house with my husband and children.

As long as I live I will never forget the thief who continues to roam the earth. He is looking for all of us from whom he can steal life away. He longs to destroy any minute traces of hope and joy. As my family's generational conflicts continue to play out, my prayer is this: I want to have the strength to snatch everything evil would consider its own prize and bring it into the presence of my Father. God says <u>all</u> things work together for good to those who love Him. I trust Him to make it happen. My earthly father's trial will be ongoing throughout 2003. How I long for the prayers of the faithful! I will enter the courtrooms with praises on my breath and singing in my heart for the beauty of my Father's holiness and for the wondrous works He has shown us. If the thief sends evil, I will take it directly to the throne for my Lord to plow through it and remake it to bring honor and glory to Himself.

During those days when heartache is touching my life, I will never forget the day of my rescue – the day the thief thought he had won. My heart will always sing a song about the right hand – a song God gave me once again as His Banah promise went to work in my life.

BANAH

The Right Hand

Knees bent, head bowed.
Humbled,
yet crumpled.
Down there in humility –
circumstance climbed on top.
Everything clogged –
grief stopped speech –
the cry was choked –
the drowning began.
But there was a flutter of the hand!
As if on its own,
with no help from the broken spirit –
The right hand fluttered like a butterfly and
took flight –
Weakly, haltingly, it rose up –
Straight up –
High above the bowed head.
The right hand –
high above the crumpled clay that couldn't
lift it on its own!
You drew it up, Lord!
The right hand held by your righteousness
–
Raising me –
from crumpled to praise.
The right hand had a life of its own that day
–
Your life, lord,
in me –
raising me once again
from the ends of the earth to Your truth!
May I never forget the right hand –
I will not fear –

I will not be dismayed – I will not boast.
My butterfly member will flutter to life
and rise up to be held –
Enfolded by your love –
Where miracles begin.

And once again,
Praise Him for His plan,
Praise Him for His provision,
Praise Him for His peace,
And praise Him for the Right Hand!

        Love in Christ,

            Angie